The biography of

George

Clooney

D1014049

The biography of

George Clooney

Andy Dougan

B◆**XTREE**

First published in 1997 by Boxtree
an imprint of Macmillan Publishers Ltd
25 Eccleston Place, London SW1W 9NF
and Basingstoke

Associated companies throughout the world

ISBN 07522 1195 1

Text © Andy Dougan 1997

10 9 8 7 6 5 4 3 2 1

A CIP catalogue entry for this book is available from the British Library.

Cover design by Shoot That Tiger!
Designed by Blackjacks
Typeset by SX Composing DTP, Rayleigh, Essex
Printed and bound in Great Britain by
Mackays of Chatham plc, Chatham, Kent

Contents

To Christine, Iain and Stuart

Acknowledgements

A s is always the case, this book would not have been possible without the help and co-operation of a number of people. I would like to thank the people of Augusta in Kentucky for their courtesy and patience, and in particular I would like to thank Bill Case and Laura Laycock. I would also like to thank Kristine Krueger of the National Film Information Service in Los Angeles and the staff at the Information Department of the British Film Institute for their help with my research. I am also grateful to Robert Rodriguez, Lawrence Bender, Gerry Lewis and Kate Lee. Finally, my thanks to Charlie Carman at Boxtree and, as always, to my agent, Jane Judd.

Chapter 1: Baby Talk

There are a number of theories by which those in the film industry conduct their daily lives. One of the most common is the doctrine of 'OMF'. In this case OMF stands for Others Must Fail. The mantra of those who follow this principle is that 'it is not enough that I succeed, others must fail'. It's the sort of philosophy perfectly illustrated by the Robert Altman film *The Player*.

George Clooney has never subscribed to this theory. The star of *ER* and the latest actor to be fitted for Batman's cape and cowl has become a household name by virtue of being the nice guy, the man for whom everyone has a good word. He has an entirely different view of how one should proceed with a career. His career has been guided by what he calls the 'And then tragedy struck' theory.

'If you ever watched *This is Your Life* on television,' he explains, 'Harold Lloyd would be on it and it would be "Harold Lloyd! You owned all the studios, and life was going great – and then tragedy struck." Or maybe it would be "Charlie Chaplin! You were the king of the world – and then tragedy struck." You can't find anyone in the world that tragedy doesn't strike,' he reasons.

John Travolta became a major star almost overnight in 1978 with the back to back successes of *Saturday Night Fever* and *Grease*. But, almost as quickly as his star rose, it fell again. A series of bad choices with films like *Moment by Moment*, the misguided *Saturday Night Fever* sequel *Staying Alive*, and the just plain awful *Two of a Kind* left him running the risk of being almost a footnote in Hollywood history.

Travolta is now a major star again thanks to *Pulp Fiction* and the sort of comeback that Lazarus would envy. But *Pulp Fiction* was actually Travolta's second comeback. His first came in 1989 with the sleeper hit *Look Who's Talking*, in which Travolta played a cabby who fell in love with single mother Kirstie Alley and eventually became a surrogate dad to her little boy Mikey. The gimmick which made *Look Who's Talking* successful was that baby Mikey 'talked', or at least Bruce Willis provided a voice-over commentary for the thoughts of Mikey.

Look Who's Talking had been successful enough to command a sequel – there were three movies in all – but it was also the inspiration for one of the most dismal sitcoms ever to appear on American television. The show was called *Baby Talk* and it starred George Clooney in what was effectively the Travolta role.

By 1991 when he was starring in *Baby Talk*, Clooney was a well-known TV face in America. He was widely tipped for stardom but had never yet quite managed to grab hold of the brass ring. And whatever else it was, *Baby Talk* certainly wasn't the brass ring.

Clooney is from a show-business background and he is steeped in cautionary tales of how the magic of fame and fortune can turn to dust almost overnight. He would not, for example, have been surprised to see what had happened to Travolta's career after that early promise. It is a classic example of his theory.

For George Clooney the summer of 1991 was one of the hardest times of his life. Although he was perennially tipped to be the mythical 'next big thing', nothing was ever coming of it. His dreams of being a movie actor were not materialising, it seemed he had yet to appear in a film which did not have the word '*Return*' in the title. Many of his films were not even being released, some went straight to video, others disappeared altogether. And although he was extremely well paid for his television work he was feeling trapped. He was, as a fellow actor who knew him then described him, 'the best-paid unknown actor in the business'.

His life it seemed was destined to revolve around short-lived sitcoms, recurring guest appearances, and pilots which were never picked up. In addition his personal life was in pretty poor shape. His brief marriage to actress Talia Balsam was in difficulty, he was in bad shape physically and mentally, and *Baby Talk* was an absolute bomb.

'It wasn't a good show to say the least,' Clooney concedes, ' and I wasn't very good in it, in fairness to the show. I had a bleeding ulcer. I wasn't well at all. I was really sick, in fact I thought I was going to die. Everything was going wrong physically and my marriage was in trouble.

And there was a man named Ed Weinberger who was the executive producer of the show who is not a nice man in my opinion.'

Clooney's opinion of Weinberger is not one which is held in isolation. Weinberger is a contentious and confrontational producer whose adversarial style tends to rub people up the wrong way. Clooney is a thoroughly professional actor who will do almost anything to get the job done regardless of personal cost. Clooney would later describe Weinberger as a man who systematically destroys people and then brags about it. There was a meanness about Weinberger, claims Clooney, that he had never encountered in almost 25 years in show business.

A confrontation between the easy-going but professional Clooney and the abrasive Weinberger, who had reportedly even fired babies from the show, was inevitable and it came one afternoon on the set. According to Clooney, Weinberger had exercised his penchant for writing pink slips by sacking an actress without even having the grace to tell her. The first the poor woman knew of it was when she turned up on the set after lunch and found her replacement reading her lines. Not surprisingly the woman burst into tears. This was enough for Clooney. 'Ed,' he says in his version of the story, 'that's enough. You don't pull that shit. You don't treat people like that.'

Weinberger was incensed at the temerity of anyone standing up to him in such a manner. What exactly happened next is a matter of interpretation. Clooney has told the story with different dialogue on different occasions but the broad gist is always the same. The actor says he stood up for his colleague and the rest of the cast and Weinberger generally badmouthed him. But Clooney refused to back down.

Clooney was not one to pick a fight but this was different. This was the way he had been raised, to stand up for yourself and – when you can – to stand up for others as well. The experience, he remembers, was curiously liberating. 'There is,' he remembers, ' the moment where you are two men sitting in a room. Now do you want to fuck with me? Forget that you're the executive producer who could fire me, because my job is already out the window. You have nothing over me now. Now I own you. Now I am bigger than you.'

To be fair to Weinberger, his version of the incident is vastly different from Clooney's. He remembers one confrontation in which the actor refused to do something in a scene having successfully done it the day before. Weinberger then maintains that it was Clooney who began using inappropriate language at a time when there were children on the set. 'If he makes it sound as though he is some kind of hero in defence of some actress, then he is going to break his arm patting himself on the back,' says Weinberger. The producer does concede that there were disagreements and arguments, and he admits that Clooney is an actor he does not get along with.

Something had to give and in the end it was Clooney. He did something he had never done before or since and left the show. To be honest he was jumping before being pushed, since there was no way any television producer would tolerate that kind of confrontation with as expendable a commodity as a handsome male actor.

For Clooney it seemed that his theory had been borne out. Tragedy had struck and the blow was all the more ironic for having been delivered because he was standing up for somebody else. At the very least he was probably facing a law suit for breach of contract from Columbia Television and probably another from the ABC network. In addition Weinberger was making good on the age-old threat to ensure that Clooney would never work in that town again. He was being quoted in trade papers to the effect that Clooney was trouble and should not be hired. Clooney also claims that Weinberger even phoned the ABC network bosses and said that the actor had physically threatened him during the confrontation.

'It was a very bad time for me,' says Clooney looking back. 'Ed and I, we had different ideas of how to do a television show. His idea was to be mean to everyone and my idea was that I didn't want to come to work like that. So I quit the show. I remember calling my agent and I said "What happens if I walk away from this? Do I end my career now?" Because when you're an actor you can only see about that far ahead,' he explains. 'And my agent was honest with me. He said "I don't know." And I thought "You know what? It's worth it." That was probably the best time for me, because that was when I really did have something to lose. And when I walked away, I walked away for all the right reasons and I did the right thing. That was literally the day I changed my life. I changed everything from that day on.'

Things were looking bad for Clooney but a short time after the Weinberger row there was a chink of hope when he was asked by an unknown writer-director to try out for a low-budget thriller movie. The writer-director was Quentin Tarantino, the movie was *Reservoir Dogs*, and Clooney blew the audition big time. The chink of hope had shut as quickly as it opened. He and Tarantino have since become good friends and the director ribs him mercilessly about his dismal audition for the film which launched Tarantino's career. Clooney can join in the fun now but at the time he found it far from amusing.

Although Clooney anticipated the worst, it never happened. There was no law suit, either from Columbia or from ABC, and instead Clooney actually found himself looked on as something of a folk hero in the close-knit community of American television. He was the man who had stood up to Ed Weinberger. He was the guy in the schoolyard who had finally stood up to the school bully. There were those who felt that Weinberger had had it coming to him for some time and they were more than happy blithely to ignore his threats that Clooney would never work again.

Clooney in fact was out of work for less than a week. 'I got a job within four days,' he explains. 'It was a pilot with Gary David Goldberg. It was called *Knights of the Kitchen Table* and it was probably one of the best pilots I had ever done but it wasn't picked up. I met Gary and the executive producer just as Ed had printed something in the paper saying I would never work again. I kept getting calls because what I didn't know was that Ed had apparently been banned from every set on every show. He was banned from the *Cosby* set, banned from *Amen*, banned from *Dear John*. All of these people hated him. 'So I got a call from Gary and the producer of *Knights of the Kitchen Table* four days later. I told them I thought I was too old for the part. "No problem," they said, "we'll make him older." I asked them why they were doing this and they said for the simple reason that it would be fun for them to do that to Ed Weinberger. So that was fun.'

No matter how much he enjoyed the experience there is no getting away from the fact that *Knights of the Kitchen Table* was another of Clooney's failed pilots. But the Weinberger incident had changed him. He was now his own man, he was taking charge of his life. And one way of doing that was by accepting what he was doing. Clooney realised that he didn't have to do 'B' movies to become a movie star. He became aware that most of the biggest movie stars around – even Clint Eastwood – had started their careers in television. John Travolta, whose role he had been playing in *Baby Talk*, had started out on the hit TV series *Welcome Back Kotter*. The trick lay in choosing the right kind of television. There would be no more 'B' movies and no more dud sitcoms for Clooney. He would use his television fame to build a movie career but it would be done gradually. He would go the way of Mickey Rourke and Alec Baldwin who carefully moved from platform to platform as they went from memorable small roles, in *Body Heat* and *Beetlejuice* respectively, to becoming major movie stars.

All it required was the right part. Three years later, in the summer of 1994, George Clooney finally grabbed the brass ring. He turned down the chance of a starring role in one pilot to play a featured role in the ensemble cast of a pilot medical show written by Michael Crichton and produced by Steven Spielberg.

ER made George Clooney a household name in a matter of weeks. Within months he was an international sex symbol, and within two years he was poised to be the first superstar of the new millennium.

Chapter 2:
Nick and Nina

Maysville in Kentucky is a typical example of small-town America. The town is in the northernmost part of Kentucky, almost on the border with Ohio. Although it retains its small-town atmosphere the growth of the nearest major city Cincinnati means that Maysville has largely been swallowed by Greater Cincinnati, a 45-minute drive to the north.

It is still the sort of place where everybody knows everyone else. But in the Forties, when it was much smaller, it was the sort of place where it's easy to get yourself noticed. The Clooneys of Maysville certainly managed to do that. Everyone knew them and everyone had them marked down as a family who might make their mark in the world one day.

It was the Clooney children who attracted most of the attention. There were the girls – Rosemary and Betty, good-looking girls and talented singers – and Nick, a charming boy who was a good listener and an even better talker. They were talented, they were popular and almost everyone agreed that with a bit of luck they might be able to make something of themselves in the entertainment industry.

In fact the Clooneys were second generation showbiz. Their Uncle George was a local radio star and war hero. He had cut a dashing figure as a bomber pilot in World War Two and had come back home to land a job at a local radio station where his easy charm and snappy patter made him a popular presenter. The young Clooneys hero-worshipped Uncle George. When their own parents divorced it was Uncle George who became the major influence in their life. It was also Uncle George who recognised the emerging talents in the family.

It was obvious that Nick, who adored his uncle, was prime showbiz material. As well as listening to Uncle George as he grew up, Nick Clooney's other great hero was the broadcasting legend Edward R. Murrow. Nick Clooney wasn't sure which of them he most wanted to be like but he knew that he would be a broadcaster when he got older.

It was the girls though who had the real talent. Rosemary and Betty had started singing on local radio when Rosemary was just thirteen and Betty only ten. Uncle George recognised their abilities and persuaded them to go on the road with him as their manager. They sang in a number of bands throughout the state and quickly became local headliners. Betty, however, couldn't take life on the road and decided that she wanted some sort of normality in her life. She quit when she was only thirteen, leaving Rosemary to go solo. Again under Uncle George's guidance she moved to New York, became an instant hit with her recording of *Come-on-a-My House*, and went on to become one of America's best loved singing stars of the Forties and Fifties. Rosemary Clooney sang with Sinatra and Bing Crosby and was an enormous success. Her records sold millions and she won fifteen gold discs. Her face was on the cover of magazines all over America as she became something of a pin-up. Like so many of her contemporaries she managed to parlay her singing success into a brief movie career. She starred in five movies in 1953 and 1954, one of which – *White Christmas* – has become an enduring classic.

Nick, meanwhile, had stayed behind in Kentucky to build a career in broadcast journalism. Those were the great days of radio and Clooney's natural charm and ready wit made him an instant success. Influenced undoubtedly by Murrow and his famous wartime broadcasts from blitz-hit London, Nick Clooney desperately wanted to be a newscaster, as they were called in those pre-anchor man days. He began his career in Lexington in Kentucky and quickly became a popular and influential local journalist. His popularity was such that he was elected president of the Bluegrass Press Club, an indication of the respect in which he was held in the industry and the community.

As a local broadcasting celebrity, one of his more pleasant duties was to act as master of ceremonies for the Miss Lexington beauty pageant. The contest winner in 1959 was an attractive student from the University of Kentucky and it was also Nick's job to chaperone her to her various official functions. 'By about the fifth or sixth of those chicken-and-peas dinners, I said, "Would you please pass the butter and would you marry me,"' recalls Nick Clooney. 'She picked up the butter, looked at it for a second and said "Here's the butter, and okay."'

Two months later Nick and Nina Clooney were married in Lexington.

Nick Clooney had acquired a wife and before long he was the proud father of two children. First there was a daughter, Ada, and then on May 6, 1961, their second child was born. It was a boy and they named him after Uncle George. George Clooney was born in the Year of the Ox, according to the Chinese calendar. People born in those years are said to be characterised by their loyalty, a quality which George Clooney would demonstrate many times in the years when he was struggling to be a success.

Young George was a charming child. He inherited his mother's beauty – he has her eyes and nose – and his father's verve and vigour. He was active and energetic and full of life. He loved to laugh and he loved to make others laugh too. A picture of him at the age of three shows a mop-topped tyke with a huge grin interrupted only by two prominent front teeth. He is dressed in a hooded sweatshirt, the drawstrings pulled tight framing his face, and wearing a pair of working trousers which appear to be several sizes too large. The trouser bottoms have been turned up several times. But it is the grin which is the most notable thing about the child. Even in a grainy black and white photograph it shines like a beacon. This is plainly a happy little boy.

Although he managed to build a successful career, Nick Clooney felt keenly the effects of the break-up of his own parents' marriage. He and Rosemary and Betty had never really known a proper family environment; they had all been very young when their parents split up. They were separated for most of their early lives and Nick Clooney was deter-mined that no matter what, he and Nina would do their best to provide a stable family environment for Ada and George. It couldn't have been easy for the Clooneys. By the nature of things Nick's was a fickle line of work and one in which he was only ever judged to be as good as his last set of ratings. There were also odd hours as he hosted all sorts of chat shows at all sorts of stations. It was difficult to give his kids the attention that other fathers might. There was, however, a simple solution. 'I was determined that my kids shouldn't suffer the way that I and my sisters had suffered,' remembers Nick. 'That's why I took them to work with me all the time. I just couldn't stand to be away from them for any length of time.'

Although it was an unconventional lifestyle it was a happy childhood for George and Ada and they thrived on it. And for George, if his dad wasn't there, then there was always Uncle George to step in as a surrogate father. Nick Clooney and Uncle George were the two single greatest influences on the young boy. From his father he learned his craft – the child knew his way around a broadcasting control room at the age of three – and from his Uncle George he learned not to take any nonsense and to be a stand-up guy. The lessons which George Clooney learned from his uncle were undoubtedly what shaped his behaviour in his confrontation with Ed Weinberger on the set of *Baby Talk*.

George Clooney spent all of his spare time with his father at the various radio and television stations in Ohio, Kentucky and Indiana where Nick plied his trade. Young George grew up thinking in television terms. Once, so a family legend goes, he had a throat infection and began to lose his voice. 'Papa! Papa!' he called to Nick in exasperation, 'I'm having trouble with my audio!'

The child was also a natural performer. He had a great sense of humour and loved the sound of other people laughing. And you had to be good to make yourself heard in the Clooney household with Nick, Aunt Rosemary and her Oscar-winning husband Jose Ferrer all contributing to the entertainment. 'We're very competitive,' says George Clooney. 'Everybody was trying to throw in the first one-liner.'

Another legend from those family gatherings has Nick Clooney telling a risque story until he realises that young George and other children are in the room. Doing the decent thing he attempts to censor the joke as he goes along. Everything goes just fine until he gets to the punch-line by which time he has decided simply to omit the offending word altogether. Nick stops himself just as he gets to the word in question, only for young George to supply the punchline by shouting – with impeccable timing – 'Shit!' He got such a laugh that he avoided getting into any trouble.

As for any child growing up in the Sixties, television was a huge influence on George Clooney's formative years. But television played a more important part in his life than most others. For one thing it provided his family's livelihood, his father was on television, and he knew the secrets of how the magic box worked. He knew the studio inside out and he was full of questions about the arcane arts of broadcasting.

Television also kept him in touch with his Aunt Rosemary. He could watch her movies on television and he could also see her on variety shows where she would guest with some of the biggest stars of the day. And it was television which brought George Clooney into contact with one of the most traumatic incidents in his young life.

In the summer of 1968 Rosemary Clooney was out in California campaigning on behalf of Robert Kennedy in the presidential race. Irish-

Catholic to their backbone, the Clooneys were staunch Kennedy supporters and Rosemary Clooney was one of a number of celebrities out on the stump for the former Attorney-General. As the brother of America's most charismatic chief executive, who had been assassinated almost five years previously, Bobby Kennedy was a shoo-in for the Presidency until he himself was shot by Sirhan Sirhan on June 5. He died in hospital the following day. The full horror of the shooting was captured on television. As the fateful events unfolded out in California Nick Clooney was back in Cincinnati watching in mounting horror. George was watching with him and he noticed his father crying in front of the screen.

Even at a tender age George guessed what was going on. He turned and ran into his bedroom. Instead of seeking solace under the covers he simply gathered up all his toy guns, took them to his father in the TV room and told him he didn't want them any more.

That night was also George Clooney's first brush with the theory which he would later articulate as the 'And then tragedy struck' principle.

That night was the beginning of the end for his Aunt Rosemary. She had been married to Academy Award-winning actor José Ferrer for thirteen years but the marriage had ended in 1966. Her own popularity was also on the wane and she had taken comfort in various cocktails of drink and tranquillisers. The trauma of Kennedy's death in 1968 was enough to tip her over the edge and she became addicted to prescription drugs. Her public behaviour became increasingly bizarre. On one occasion in the midst of a performance in Nevada she gave up on the music and started haranguing the audience with a rant about CIA conspiracies against the Kennedys. Finally, accepting that she needed help, she checked herself into the psychiatric wing of Cedars-Sinai hospital in Los Angeles.

George Clooney was only seven years old when Auntie Rosie got sick. He was young but he was already learning that there was more to the entertainment industry than getting cheap laughs with a dirty joke.

Chapter 3:
A Talented Tot

American society in the Sixties was defined as much by television as anything else. The children of the Sixties were the first generation to see themselves growing up, thanks to television. In the Forties and Fifties it was newsreels such as *Movietone* and *The March of Time* which documented the progress of society, but in the Sixties it was television.

It was an era when television set the trends. It was an era of Davy Crockett hats, Beatles wigs and *Wagon Train* cowboy outfits. Television had supplanted radio as the country's most popular form of entertainment. Movies too were feeling the pinch and the decline of the big studios brought about by the competition from television was already under way. And television was growing too. It was accessible to more and more homes, there were now three major networks, colour was coming in, and new technology, such as broadcasting satellites like Telstar and Early Bird, constantly increased the ability of the medium to communicate its message.

The programmes were changing too. The slapstick innocence of *I Love Lucy* would give way to the more sophisticated *Lucy Show*. Writers like Carl Reiner and Mel Brooks who had cut their teeth in the Fifties with Sid Caesar on *Your Show of Shows* were now writing for programmes like *The Dick van Dyke Show*. The most popular shows on television when George Clooney was born were the big three TV westerns – *Wagon Train*, *Bonanza* and *Gunsmoke*. Ratings were enormous and in the space of a decade television would become the most powerful and influential medium the world had ever seen. Very early in that decade Americans saw for themselves, although they may not have realised it, the real power of television. One of the reasons for John F. Kennedy's victory over Richard Nixon was that he was simply more telegenic and appealing to a rapidly growing audience. Television had effectively given them a President.

The early part of the Sixties was an exciting time to be working in television in the United States. Nick Clooney was revelling in the challenge and opportunity it presented. Working out of Cincinnati he was not a major network star, nor would he ever be. But Cincinnati was a major market, in the lower half of the top twenty nationwide. The station where Clooney worked, WRW, was a big station in that market. So Nick Clooney, even though he was a big fish in a small pond, was still a household name and a popular local celebrity. As well as the television work he would also appear on local radio and had appeared in musicals at the local theatre.

George Clooney has compared his father to Cincinnati's version of Johnny Carson. Carson, who would go on to be America's king of television, was at that stage himself working on a small town television station. Doubtless he and Nick Clooney harboured the same ambitions with different results. 'My father was as big a star as you could be,' recalls Clooney. 'He was very popular and a really respected citizen in the town. He was a celebrity in that little tri-state area of Ohio, Kentucky and Indiana. He always had a show of some kind going on and he had 60 or 70 shares. That means 70 per cent of everybody who had their televisions on would watch Nick. He was God. Everybody everywhere we walked would stop him.' It's hard to imagine now the status of someone with his own television show in those days. The novelty and influence of television was such that even in a small market, a television personality could be a major local celebrity. Cincinnati was, as we have seen, not a small market. Nick Clooney's lunchtime show was one of the most popular shows on WRW. He would undoubtedly have been a man of some importance and influence in the area and it goes without saying there would have been a fair measure of reflected glory on George and Ada simply by virtue of being Nick Clooney's children. 'I was Nick Clooney's son right away, always,' George remembers. 'Believe me I'm not complaining. I really loved that attention and I loved the things that it got me to do, you get to meet a lot of people.'

The Nick Clooney Show itself was a mix of variety and chat which had more than a hint of old-time vaudeville about it. Although he had been keen to become a newscaster, like his hero Edward R. Murrow, Nick Clooney was more than happy to front the variety-talk show. However, perhaps as a concession to his original ambition, Nick would also read the main nighttime news as well. George had been visiting the studio almost before he could walk and was never in the least intimated by the technology or the paraphernalia. When his father was doing his radio show, the five-year-old George would frequently operate the control booth for him. Nick would read the weather and George would operate the microphone and occasionally chip in with the temperature. When his father was doing television, George and his sister Ada would hold cue cards and do all sorts of menial but nonetheless important jobs around the studio. But George was a natural performer, and had been since an early age, so it was only natural that he should eventually become a sort of human prop on his father's programme.

It's very easy to date George Clooney's first appearance before the cameras. 'On St Patrick's Day, when I was five years old, I put on the little green suit and stuck a cigar in my mouth and they interviewed me like I was a leprechaun,' says Clooney. 'I was also the Easter Bunny that year too.'

The cute leprechaun was an instant hit with audiences. Nick Clooney knew a good thing when he saw it and before too long George was a regular guest on the show. He would turn up about twice a week doing songs, routines and playing seasonal characters like Easter Bunnies and Christmas snowmen. If audiences loved George then advertisers would love him too. Local firms were quick to see his potential and George soon started doing commercials for diverse items like Husman's potato chips and a bizarre sounding product called Green Magic which was supposed to clean all your kitchenware and bring it up like new.

George took to his new part-time career like a duck to water. Ada, a little older, a little more serious and a little more shy, soon gave it up leaving the spotlight completely to her younger brother.

But although it was a glamorous life for a growing boy, it was also a precarious existence. The rapid and highly competitive growth of television and its immense importance to advertisers meant that ratings were more and more important. Once a show started to slip in the ratings or a sponsor withdrew support the show was finished.

A cancelled show didn't mean much to the audience, there was always something to replace it after all, but for the Clooneys a cancelled show was a disaster. When shows were pulled, that meant Dad was out of a job and it was time for the Clooneys to move on.

Once *The Nick Clooney Show* was cancelled in Cincinnati, they moved to Columbus in Ohio, a smaller station but still one which enabled them to live in some comfort. The experience in Columbus was not a particularly pleasant one for George Clooney, who was once again to encounter his theory of 'And then tragedy struck'.

Nick was fired from the station in Columbus but George and Ada only discovered it from the morning newspaper. The front page headline simply read 'Clooney Canned'. All day at school they were both teased mercilessly in the casually cruel manner of which only children are capable. Nick found them both in tears when he went to pick them up from school that afternoon. 'They had been taunted all day by the other kids,' recalls Nick Clooney. 'All day some of these kids had been shouting at them "Your Daddy's been fired." I had to hug them and explain that there would be another show but they were inconsolable. They got in the car and I thought "What should I do?"' he remembers. 'So I said "Remember when George Gobel was here last week and you had the whole class down to the station and lorded it over them? Well, there's no free lunch. When their fathers get fired no one knows about it," Nick Clooney told his tearful children. 'When you get to be famous and you get to meet all those famous faces there's a payback, and here it is.'

Times turned out to be tough in Columbus and the family moved from what had been, in comparative terms, a mansion to a trailer park. The four of them lived in the trailer and even though things were hard there were important lessons for George which would serve him well in later life. He learned from his father, as he had from Uncle George, the importance of standing your ground for something you believed in. He learned that being your own man was more important than almost anything else. 'I remember one time when my father quit a show for all the right reasons,' remembers Clooney without elaborating on the circumstances of the dispute. 'The station was playing hardball and they held the contract out on him. They wouldn't let him work within a hundred miles of Cincinnati for a year. So dad bought the contract and beat it two days before the year was up. But we were unemployed for a stretch.'

Things picked up eventually and Nick Clooney found another job in Mason, Ohio. The family was able to move out of the trailer and into another reasonable home. Then from Mason they moved back to the Bluegrass State when Nick got another job.

He was going back to being a news anchor on WKRW Channel 12 in Cincinnati. With his new job Nick decided that the family should move again, this time to Augusta in Kentucky.

The move to Augusta was not a popular one in the Clooney household. Nick was all in favour but Nina didn't especially want to go, and neither did George. But for Nick Clooney, going to Augusta was almost like going home. It was only 17 miles away from Maysville where he had grown up and it was a short drive from his new job in Cincinnati.

Augusta is a small town with a population even now which barely exceeds 1500. It would not have matched the Clooneys previous glamorous, albeit parlous, existence but it offered something more important than celebrity and glamour. Life in Augusta offered something which Nick Clooney had come to prize greatly over the years. The constant career buffeting he had suffered and the strain of keeping the family together must have exacted a price. The family was stressed out and moving to Augusta gave them a chance to catch their collective breath and put down roots. With the children approaching their teenage years Nick Clooney decided they needed a suitable environment to grow up in. So, in Augusta, after a period which George has subsequently characterised as 'moving whenever the rent was due', the Clooneys would finally find some degree of permanence and security. Nina eventually came round to the idea and she and the children soon realised that Augusta was the perfect place to live. George had been to five primary schools in eight years but in Augusta he could settle down and go to high school.

Moving from school to school could not have failed to have an impact on the young George Clooney. 'It was like *Gulliver's Travels*,' he would say later, 'I'd go from one school where I was the idiot to the next one where I was a genius.'

It would be hard enough for any child to settle down under those circumstances but for George and Ada, life was made even more difficult by the fact that their father was a famous name. Ada dealt with it in her own quiet way – she excelled academically and went on to be a National Merit scholar. But George would invariably have to prove himself in the unforgiving world of the school playground. 'We'd move into a new neighbourhood and just because of who my dad was I'd have to get into a fist fight almost immediately to prove that I wasn't a wuss,' he says. 'And I was the worst at it,' he recalls painfully. 'I was always getting my ass kicked by everybody.'

The nomadic lifestyle of that eight-year period taught George Clooney a lot about resilience and self-reliance and the transient nature of fame and success. But the move from station to station also enabled him to increase his range of broadcasting talents. By the time he was a teenager he was spending so much time around the set of his father's shows that he was even able to fill in as floor manager when the occasion demanded. He would help out on other shows that his father did, such as *Bowling for Dollars*, and would host various movie matinees. He was also continuing to appear on screen as well, making his singing debut with a version of

Straighten Up and Fly Right in a World War Two nostalgia tribute. Clooney also apparently contributed a distinctive version of the Carpenters' *Sing* in another show. Neither performance appears to have been preserved on videotape and the world can only mourn the loss of a budding musical comedy star.

For Nick Clooney, the family had been through a lot but importantly to him – and unlike his own experience with his sisters – they had stayed together throughout a difficult period. 'The important thing was that both kids were very involved in all those TV shows,' says Nick Clooney. 'George was backstage at all of them. When we were doing the show in Cincinnati, George would get on stage before the show started and warm up the audience. He even sang songs when guests were late.

'Ada passed out coffee and doughnuts but she never really cared for show business,' Clooney continues. 'But George revelled in it. He made friends with a lot of the guests, including Kenny Rogers. George was always full of questions.'

Nick Clooney's life was probably not that different from many of his colleagues. It was an uncertain blend of famine and feast. When the ratings were high then life was good, but when they were low he struggled to meet the mortgage payments. Looking back on his childhood George Clooney readily acknowledges the impermanence of his existence.

'When I was a kid,' he recalled to an interviewer, 'the numbers, and how the show was doing were what determined what you got for Christmas. Moving from a mansion in Kentucky to a trailer, and from a trailer to a nice house, gave you a sense of how quickly your career can fall apart. But also how quickly you can get it back too.'

Chapter 4: 'I'm Going to be a Star'

Going into Augusta, Kentucky, in the Seventies was a bit like travelling through a time warp. It was a bit like leaving the sexual revolution behind and heading back towards *Leave it to Beaver* territory. Augusta in the Seventies was much like the rest of America had been in the Fifties. The pace of life was much slower and life was much simpler.

Augusta was originally a farm town. It still retains a sense of the pioneer spirit which colonised the country. For example, every year on Labor Day weekend they still have a Heritage Day which celebrates their frontier antecedents. It's about 40 miles from Cincinnati – no more than a 45-minute drive – but as Cincinatti has expanded over the years it is now more like a sub-division of the big city rather than a village in its own right.

But some of the important aspects of small town Americana have survived and Augusta has retained its own separate identity and managed to avoid being swallowed up into some huge conurbation. The chief employers in the town now are the local factories which make plastics and door knobs, but there is still enough of old-fashioned America to make it the sort of place which must seem like a dream home. There is a sense of community in Augusta which is missing in so many towns; people tend not to stray too far away. Kids grow up and might work in Cincinnati but they stay in Augusta. Even though he came from Maysville, Augusta must have seemed like coming home as far as Nick Clooney was concerned.

In the village of Augusta things like hay-rides, Fourth of July picnics, Easter egg hunts and town barbecues were major social events. The local high school also figured prominently in the village's social calendar. The locals turned out in force to support the school football, baseball and basketball teams in their seasons. The annual High School prom always brought crowds of parents to the doors of the school gym to take pictures of the boys in their rented tuxedoes and the girls in their prom dresses. It may all sound a little bit like *American Graffiti* but there seems little doubt that it was a nice place to live and a nice place to bring up children. That's what appealed so much to Nick Clooney. 'It was a wonderful place to grow up,' says Nick Clooney. 'George was hard-pressed to get away with anything because all of the neighbours knew everyone else's kids and they kept an eye on them.'

They were also keeping an eye on Nick Clooney. The family's arrival in Augusta was a big event. They were far and away the most famous people in the town and there was an element of celebrity spotting when they first arrived. 'When the Clooneys moved to town it was big news,' says high school teacher Bill Case. 'Nick Clooney was the news anchor on Channel 12. You can get used to seeing someone every night on television but when you see them walking down your street then that is something.'

It's always hard for a child to settle in a new school in a strange town, as George and Ada had recently found to their cost. But Augusta was different. It had an old world Southern gentility about it. It is a village where people are naturally neighbourly and Nick Clooney must have known his children would be accepted much more easily there than they had been at some of their previous schools.

The easy charm which George had inherited from his father and the confidence he had acquired from his television appearances undoubtedly helped. So too did the fact that there were only 26 pupils in his class. Even so, having dressed up on television as a leprechaun or the Easter Bunny wasn't going to cut much ice in a new school. George Clooney was going to have to use other skills to make an impression. He chose two tried and tested methods; he made people laugh and he impressed them with his sporting prowess.

George Clooney quickly gained a reputation at Augusta High School as not just the class clown, but the school clown. The love of performing and the need to be at the centre of the action which he had shown since the age of three had not deserted him. Teacher Bill Case remembers him as the sort of pupil who 'never shied away from your attention'.

Bill Case has been teaching for 23 years. Now he teaches business studies and accounting but when he came across George Clooney in his senior year at high school in 1977 he was teaching typing. Case always believed that typing was the one skill that everyone should have and certainly Clooney would put it to good use later on as he prepared résumé after résumé for agents and casting directors.

Bill Case remembers George Clooney very well and not because he was particularly rebellious or difficult to deal with. Case is an old-fashioned teacher and Augusta is an old-fashioned town where teachers could in those days, and still can, have one to one teaching with their pupils. This was not some anonymous concrete high school building. Augusta High School dates back to the eighteenth century; it was a former Methodist College and enjoys a place in the footnotes of local history as the first of its type west of the Alleghenies.

'It's not surprising that George was memorable,' says Laura Laycock, Clooney's closest childhood friend who was a year ahead of him at Augusta High. 'In George's graduating class and in my graduating class there were only 26 pupils. We were all like brothers and sisters. As the years go by we stay in touch with classmates and teachers and everyone remembers everyone else.'

George Clooney was not especially academically gifted. Laura Laycock remembers him as being an average student, but that was probably because he wasn't as engaged academically as he might have been. He did well in things that interested him. He was a leading light in the school's Science Club for example. But if he wasn't interested then his mind would wander and he would look for pranks to play or other distractions to occupy him.

But there were signs even then that he had a fair idea of what he was going to be in later life. 'George was one kid who knew exactly what he was going to do with his life,' says Bill Case without a moment's hesitation. 'Every day in class he would tell me "I'm telling you Mr Case, you better hang on to these typing papers because I'm going to be a big movie star some day." I just used to laugh and tell them that when he did become famous I would come and get his autograph.'

Bill Case's memories of George Clooney are slightly at odds with the shy, withdrawn boy who comes across in some magazine profiles. But there appears to have been no hint of shyness in Clooney at school – the boy was born to perform and part of that has to come from being part of a family of entertainers.

It was undoubtedly the need to perform which led to all those jokes and tricks. 'George just naturally became the clown,' remembers Laura Laycock. 'Wherever George was you knew you were going to have a good time.' Other classmates still remember vintage Clooney pranks. On one

occasion he even managed to convince a teacher that a pupil was commit-
ting suicide.

Clooney had skipped his lessons and gone up to the floor above the
room where he should have been at a maths class. He took his arms, put a
shoe on each hand, and then hung down so that the shoes were facing into
the classroom. Clooney started screaming and yelling for help and generally
causing a commotion. When the maths teacher looked up to see what was
going on all he could see was what he thought was a pair of legs hanging
from an upper floor and thrashing wildly in the air, banging on the
window.The poor teacher almost fainted and in the end Clooney had to
rush downstairs and let him in on the joke.

It wasn't just the maths faculty which bore the brunt of Clooney's
sense of humour. A hapless science teacher became another unwitting patsy
in Clooney's steady rise to popularity. During a biology class, Clooney and
his classmates were supposed to be dissecting a sand shark. Clooney got
bored and saw the opportunity for another prank. He took the shark he was
dissecting off the bench and then quietly sneaked up behind the teacher.
While the teacher continued to lecture to the class, Clooney held the shark
above the teacher's head. He had slipped his hand inside and was effectively
using the shark as a glove puppet, moving the mouth in sync with what the
teacher was saying. His classmates thought it was hilarious but it's debat-
able whether the teacher would see the funny side.

Clooney's broadcasting experience also stood him in good stead in
another favourite trick. He had at that time, and still has, a talent for
mimicry. He used to impersonate teachers, friends and local characters. He
would even create whole new characters with a succession of weird voices.
The next step was to phone people at home and pretend to be the local
radio presenter. Clooney could call them up and convince them they had
won cash prizes. Very few people managed to resist his pitch and hardly
anyone failed to be taken in by it.

George Clooney quickly became one of the most popular boys in the
school and again he thrived on the attention. The boys liked him because
he was one of the lads and they never felt threatened by his success and –
as a foretaste of what was to come in his professional life – the girls were
just crazy about him. 'He definitely liked the girls,' claims Bill Case. 'I don't
think he ever had problems finding a date. I think the only problem he ever
had with girls was that there used to be so many of them lining up just to
walk home with him.'

But although he remained popular, George didn't have time for any steady dates. 'It wasn't that he was a shy boy or anything,' says Laura Laycock. 'He was very outgoing and everything like that. He didn't have a steady girlfriend through high school, in fact he didn't have many girl-friends at all, he was just friends with everyone. I don't think he wanted to pick one girl out ahead of the others. George always liked to go to parties and be with his friends and he always had a good time. But there really wasn't an awful lot to do at that time. We would just spend our evenings, the whole group of us, cruising around in our cars.'

There was more to George Clooney than just a succession of not always innocent pranks. He was beginning to find other things he was good at. Any youthful testosterone which might have been channelled towards the young female population in Augusta was being dissipated in another direction. George Clooney had discovered sports in a big way.

'He was a good ball player,' remembers Bill Case. 'He played almost every sport there was going. But given that the school was so small, once the kids had reached the age when they were mature enough to play sports you were only picking from about 18 or 20 boys.'

Even by those standards George was starting to excel at sports. He played football and basketball but his first love was baseball. He was rapidly becoming the big man on what was, to be sure, a very small campus. Pictures of Clooney at the time show that he was filling out nicely. A tallish, rangy, open-faced young man, he never seemed to be photographed with-out that smile that would break millions of hearts all over the world.

Every American boy dreams of being a baseball star and George Clooney was no different. They dream of following in the footsteps of the greats; men like Mickey Mantle and Joe Di Maggio, or – more recently – Cal Ripken or Dave Whitfield or Roger Clemens. They dream of hitting match-winning home runs for their home-town team while their family and friends sit cheering in the bleachers. Unlike most young boys, George Clooney came frustratingly close to realising that dream.

By the time he was 16 it was obvious that the boy was more than just a good high school ball player. He began to attract the attention of scouts for various professional organisations within Major League Baseball. Clooney was making something of a name for himself in the mid-West. Eventually, during the pre-season training of 1978, he got the call from the famous Cincinnati Reds. Clooney was being given the chance to emulate his great hero Willie Mays and he was keen to take it. Bill Case recalls, however, that good and all as he was, Clooney wasn't the obvious choice. 'George wasn't the best player on the team,' Case maintains. 'There was a boy there who was even better than George and I used to encourage him to go for a trial with the Reds but he never did.'

Clooney had a reputation as a big hitter. He was the sort of batter who could knock the cover off the ball and send it flying to any corner of the field. His trial for the Reds would find out whether there was more to him than just being a power hitter – they wanted to see if he could be a baseball player. He wanted to play centre field, a position which requires a degree of completeness from a baseball player unlike any other on the team. Unfortunately for Clooney, what would in effect be his first bigtime audition did not go well. The Reds coaches found out that what their scouts had told them was true – the kid could certainly belt the ball. But that was all he could do. His speed between the bases was suspect and his throwing arm was non-existent. This meant he could bat but he couldn't really field and, as far as the Reds were concerned, he was only half a ball player.

It goes without saying that George Clooney was devastated. At the age of 16 he felt, as all boys of that age do when things go wrong, that his life was over. More importantly for him, he had no idea what he now wanted to do. He had set his heart on a being a professional ball player to the exclusion of everything else, specifically playing centre field for the Cincinnati Reds. Clooney had made it quite plain to his father that he didn't really have any interest in going into television. Since he seemed to spend more time in school joking than studying he was not well prepared academically for college life.

George Clooney graduated from high school without much of a clue of what he was going to do after that. He had invested all his hopes in the Cincinnati Reds and they had passed him over. Even that great American rite of passage, the high school prom, was about to pass him by. The high school prom was one of the great social events in the Augusta calendar and George Clooney didn't have a date.

The Clooneys and the Laycocks were near neighbours in Augusta and had become friends. The Laycocks' daughter Laura was a year older than George. She was in her freshman year at college when George was graduating from high school. The two had been friends – Laura describes herself as having been something of a tomboy in those days – but they were only pals, there was no romantic attachment. It was Laura Laycock who accompanied George Clooney to the high school prom and rescued him from social embarrassment. But she was the one who had to make all the running.

'Our families were friends, we were friends, and so I asked George to be my date,' she remembers. 'I wasn't surprised he didn't have a date because, like I say, I don't remember him dating a single special girl in high school. He had friends, and some of those friends were girls, but I don't remember him ever having a lover.'

So on the first Saturday in May 1977 George Clooney and Laura Laycock went to the August High School prom. They met up with a bunch of friends beforehand and they were snapped, along with all the other happy couples, by the crowds of parents standing outside the dance hall. Laura's souvenir photograph shows George resplendent in a silver-grey three-piece suit with satin lapels and trim. This being the Seventies his dress shirt has a huge lace ruff, and his matching grey bow-tie is about the size of a butterfly from the Amazonian rainforest. Laura is wearing a simple but elegant long white dress. She has a peach-coloured corsage pinned to the left shoulder of her dress, George has a matching peach coloured rose in his button-hole. As they pose together with their arms round each other they are both facing squarely out of the picture. They are looking at the camera rather than each other; it is plainly a photograph of two good friends having a great time in each other's company.

The High School prom is only the centrepiece of a night-long round of events. After the dance at the school itself there are the post-prom celebrations, a round of parties which can put Oscar night to shame. George and Laura and their school friends went from party to party. 'He was having a great time,' she recalls. 'He was teasing people and doing imitations of our friends. He was just generally goofing around.'

Eventually, as dawn was breaking and the parties were winding down, the celebrations were over and a still exhilarated Clooney took Laura Laycock back to his house. 'George was the perfect gentleman, just like I knew he would be,' says Laura. 'We finished up at his house for breakfast and he gave me a shy, thank-you kiss on the cheek. It was more like a brother and sister thing.'

Chapter 5:
The Starting Line

George Clooney left high school in 1977 in something of a daze. It had been fun but it had hardly prepared him for the rest of his life. At the age of 16 his ambition had not extended much beyond playing centre field for the Cincinnati Reds and with that gone he had no idea what he was going to do next.

Despite what he had said in Bill Case's typing class he had no serious inkling of following his ultimate career path at that stage. Performing was just something he had done on his dad's show – it was fooling around, it was for amusing your friends and scoring points in school. It wasn't really a serious career. His father, however, believes that the seeds of his eventual career had already been sown by that stage. 'George had an incredible sense of humour and he was the funniest kid in town,' he remembers. 'He was clearly developing his skills as an actor even when he was in high school.'

And although he was by now a somewhat spirited young man when it came to partying and playing pranks, Nick and Nina Clooney knew that their youngster was basically good at heart. 'He drank too many beers at parties a few times like other boys will do,' his father concedes, 'but he never smoked pot or even cigarettes.'

Although George may not have had a clue about his future, he got his first taste of what it might have been like in that summer when he graduated from Augusta High School. America celebrated its bicentennial in 1976 with an orgy of well-deserved self-congratulation. Everyone it seemed got into the act. The celebrations inspired the best-selling novelist James A. Michener to write a book about what was, after all, still a young country.

Centennial would focus on the first 100 years of American history and its pioneering traditions. In the mid-Seventies, the mini-series was king on American television. The trend had been started by Irwin Shaw's *Rich Man, Poor Man*, which had screened in 1976 to astonishing ratings and made a star of Nick Nolte in the process.

After *Rich Man, Poor Man* it seemed like every epic novel in print was being turned into a mini-series by the television networks. *Centennial* was a natural and by coincidence Augusta, Kentucky, was the natural place to film it.

'The filming of *Centennial* was a real big event in Augusta,' remembers Bill Case. 'It meant a lot to this town, there was real excitement. They put adverts in all the papers for people to come along and try out as extras and a lot of the high school seniors went along.' Among them, not surprisingly, was George Clooney. Laura Laycock went with him.

'They chose Augusta for *Centennial* because of the river front,' explains Laura Laycock. 'Apart from the river itself, there are no utility cables or power stations or anything else along there so it hasn't changed much. We also have a lot of very old Southern houses here and there are a lot of antique and craft shops so that's why they filmed it here. They were asking all sorts of people if they wanted to be in it as extras. We were all just teenagers then so we all said "Yes", and that's how we got the parts. No one got any speaking parts, we were just walking up and down the streets as extras.'

A picture of George and his friends taken on the set shows the 17-year-old Clooney dressed in a tricorn hat and faux pioneer garb with a group of his friends, including Laura Laycock. Some are sporting some very un-18th century Foster Grants but they all appear to be having a great time.

Centennial was good fun and a diverting way of spending the summer. But with the new academic term approaching and George not having much of an idea of what he wanted to do, Nick Clooney was adamant that his son should make something of himself. The nomadic existence of a professional broadcaster had instilled in him a sense of the need for some kind of qualification to fall back on. Nick Clooney knew that his son certainly had the practical experience to make it as a broadcaster – he knew his way round a studio almost blindfold by this stage – but broadcasting had changed. It was no longer enough simply to have the gift of the gab – you would need a degree these days. It was Nick Clooney who insisted that George go to college, and he was prepared to pay for it too. Some of George's friends were going to Northern Kentucky University and he went along with them.

The social life at Northern Kentucky suited Clooney just fine but he and the academic life were not suited to each other at all. 'To George, school was a very large restaurant and night-club,' says his mother Nina Clooney in a statement which hints at a whole world of resignation and disappointment.

Clooney notionally majored in journalism at Northern Kentucky, but his real majors appear to have been partying and drinking. The teenage party animal from Augusta threw himself into fraternity life with a gusto which should not really have come as a surprise to anyone.

They say that God created alcohol to stop the Irish from taking over the world. The Clooneys are Irish to their familial backbone. George Clooney may have swarthy, almost Mediterranean, good looks but if you cut him he would probably bleed green. The stereotypical fondness for a tipple runs strongly in the Clooney family and George was doing his best to keep his end up while he was in college. 'I can drink, I can drink with the best of them,' he would say later. 'But I'm not even in the same league as most of my family members. Almost everyone in my family, at one time or another, has been a drug addict or an alcoholic,' he admitted with remarkable candour.

The world was being made well aware of the problems in the Clooney family through the person who, at that time, was the most visible member of the clan. The breakdown which Rosemary Clooney had suffered just after Bobby Kennedy's assassination in 1968 had been the start of a long downward spiral of substance abuse. By 1977 she was in recovery and sharing her ordeal with the world in an autobiography called *This for Remembrance*. The book was eventually turned into an NBC movie called *Rosie: The Rosemary Clooney Story* with Sondra Locke in the title role. Everyone remembered Rosemary Clooney from *White Christmas*. She was the girl next door; she was the girl every American mother of the Fifties had hoped their son might bring home. And she was on drugs.

All things considered, this could not have been a happy period for the family. As well as coping with Rosemary's revelations, Nick was still trying to deal with the death of his sister Betty, who had died suddenly in 1976 from an aneurysm. Uncle George was still continuing his larger than life existence as a garrulous alcoholic. Meanwhile George was carrying on the 'family tradition' by having a wild time in college. Clooney's behaviour and his obvious lack of success at college must have added to the strain on his parents at this time.

Despite the partying, life at college was just not working out for George. After three years he was still a freshman, a poor student but an accomplished carouser. Eventually salvation arrived in the shape of the Californian branch of the Clooney clan.

One of the factors which had tipped Rosemary Clooney over the edge and into her breakdown had been the end of what had ultimately been a difficult marriage to José Ferrer. Ferrer was born in Puerto Rico and was an actor with a formidable reputation. On Broadway he was a director and producer as well as an actor. He delivered an acclaimed Iago to Paul Robeson's *Othello* in 1942 and three years later he won a Tony award for the title role in Rostand's *Cyrano de Bergerac*. He soon translated his Broadway fame into a movie career, making his debut in 1948 in *Joan of Arc* for which he was nominated for a Best Supporting Actor award. Other landmark performances included the defending officer in *The Caine Mutiny* and a sadistic Turkish commander in *Lawrence of Arabia*. He also directed a number of films, none of them especially memorable.

Ferrer and Rosemary Clooney had married in 1953. It was her first marriage; he had previously been married to the actress Uta Hagen. He was 16 years older than she. The following year they appeared in a film together when she took a guest-starring role in *Deep in My Heart*, in which Ferrer played the composer Sigmund Romberg. That was also the year, 1954, in which their first child was born. On the surface José Ferrer and Rosemary Clooney were the perfect couple; they had five children altogether. But there were cracks beneath the surface of their marriage and they split up in 1966. Rosemary Clooney started taking pills to cope with the strain and quickly became an addict.

Although Rosemary was living on the coast and the rest of the family were in the mid-West they remained close. George was friendliest with his cousin Miguel, the oldest of Rosemary's children, and seven years older than himself. Miguel Ferrer has gone on to be a fine character actor with memorable roles in *RoboCop* and *Twin Peaks* – the TV series and the film – to his credit but in the Seventies his big love was music.

He had wanted to play the drums ever since he saw Ringo Starr during the Beatles' landmark *Ed Sullivan Show* appearance in 1964. Ferrer was talented and was able to make a successful career as a professional musician before he was out of his teens. Much in demand as a session man, he was one of three drummers – one of the others was Ringo Starr – chosen by Keith Moon of The Who to play on his solo album. At that stage Moon was recognised as the world's best rock drummer.

It was Ferrer's talent as a drummer which led to his acting debut in 1975. He was close friends with Billy Mumy – now starring in *Babylon 5* but best remembered as Will Robinson from *Lost in Space* – who was appearing in a short-lived NBC sitcom called *Sunshine*. One episode called for a drummer and Mumy got the job for his old pal. Ferrer was as talented an actor as he was a drummer and never looked back.

In 1982 they were making a movie about horse racing. The movie was called *And They're Off* and it starred José Ferrer and two of his sons – Miguel and Rafael. There's really only one place to shoot a film about breeding race horses and that is Kentucky, which is responsible for some of the world's finest thoroughbreds. So the Clooney in-laws found themselves in Lexington making a movie and renewing family ties.

George Clooney by this time was 21 years old and had grown increasingly frustrated with life at Northern Kentucky University. Academically he was not shining and the money his father had given him to go to college had just about run out. He was doing a little theatre and a little broadcasting, but with the very serious prospect of flunking out looming on the horizon he was now having to give some real thought to what he would do next. One option was a career in broadcasting and, despite his initial opposition to the idea, Clooney seemed to be coming round to the realisation that this was just about the only way he could make a living. He had managed to find himself some part-time freelance work at a local TV station and was seriously considering trying to parlay that into a career.

'At that time I wanted to be the host of a television show called *PM Magazine*,' remembers Clooney. 'I was just trying to get some kind of broadcasting job. And I went down to Lexington where Miguel and his father were shooting the movie to do a story on them.'

What happened next is straight out of a movie script. Indeed if it appeared in a film script it would be rejected as being far too fanciful for anyone to believe it.

'They got me a part in the movie,' says Clooney. 'I stayed with the movie and left the part-time broadcasting job. It wasn't even a job really, it was just freelancing,' he says by way of justifying his sudden decision.

Clooney had gone to Lexington at his cousin Miguel's urging. Ferrer had told him that despite his failure at college he was still young. Why didn't he come and give this thing a run, suggested Ferrer. Neither Clooney nor Ferrer thought that anything would come of it as a career. At the very least, though, the chance to do a location piece with the film that was shooting in the area might improve George's chances of turning his part-time freelance work at the TV station into something more permanent.

The trip to Lexington changed George Clooney's life. It was like a door had opened on a whole new world of possibilities. He had been thrown a lifeline at the very last minute. Just when he was about to embark on a second choice career George Clooney was given the opportunity to do the one thing he knew he had really wanted all his life. It was even better than he had ever dreamed it would be. He had been well and truly hooked and he was having the best time of his life.

'He came and camped out in my hotel room for about three months,' says Miguel Ferrer, after Clooney had given up on college and a broadcasting career. 'We played practical jokes, we drank too much, and we had sex with about a million women.'

Obviously Ferrer is exaggerating but behind the hyperbole is the very real fact that George Clooney had finally found what he was looking for. He had found a job which was completely in sync with his own rhythms. This was a place where he could stand up and be the centre of attention and not have to yield his place to anyone.

If this had been a movie, Clooney's role in *And They're Off* would of course have led to overnight stardom and he would never have looked back. In the real world things have to be kept in perspective. We're not talking about Ruby Keeler in *42nd Street*. It wasn't a question of going out there a nobody and coming back a star. Indeed it would be an exaggeration to describe his appearance in one small scene of a low-budget movie even as a part. But it had done its job for George Clooney and there was no way he was ever going to go back to anything else after this. 'I fell in love with the whole industry,' Clooney says simply. 'I never thought I'd make any money at it but I just loved doing it. I loved the attention. It was very seductive. There were all these beautiful women paying attention to all these guys in the movie. Then the director is saying things like "You ought to be an actor too," and I'm thinking "Well, yeah, maybe I should be an actor." Finally I'd found something I was really and truly interested in.'

But although he says that money was not the prime motivation, there was another reason for the enthusiasm with which he embraced this new career possibility. 'I was very jealous of my cousins and the life they lived in California,' he admits. 'In my estimation they were rich, although I don't think they were. I remember seeing the tennis court and the pool and thinking it was just amazing.'

It's important to bear in mind that Clooney himself was not exactly dirt poor. There were times when his father had been out of work and the money had been tight, but equally there had been times when they were living high on the hog in big houses of their own. Clooney, whose father had been a big fish in a middle-size pond, was now getting an inkling of what it must be like to be a really big fish, and he liked the idea.

George Clooney's movie debut is lost in the mists of cinematic oblivion. *And They're Off* was never released, although doubtless some enterprising soul will dig it up, acquire the rights and release it on video with Clooney's name above the title one of these days. Even if no one saw it, that didn't really matter to George Clooney. He had found what he wanted to do. He wanted to be an actor.

But he couldn't be an actor in Kentucky. There would never be enough work to let him have tennis courts and swimming pools. There was only one place to go for that kind of life. George Clooney was going to Hollywood.

Chapter 6:
Family Troubles

After three years of drifting aimlessly in college George Clooney had finally found something that he wanted to do with his life. He couldn't wait to tell his parents. He reasoned, as all children do, that they would be thrilled with the news and share his enthusiasm. He couldn't have been further from the truth. When he broke the news to his father, Nick Clooney told him bluntly that if he went to Los Angeles then he would fail.

'When George said he was going to go to Hollywood to be an actor, I told him he was crazy,' says Nick Clooney. 'The rejection you suffer is very cruel and unusual. You are either too tall or too short, too fat or too thin, too this or too that – it's asking for a lifetime of rejection. But like most kids,' Clooney adds philosophically, 'George ignored his dad and did exactly what he wanted to do.'

George Clooney was stung by his parents' rejection of his career plans. Acting was what he really wanted to do. He had perhaps been joking back in school when he told Bill Case to hang on to his typing papers because he was going to be a movie star one day, but now it was the real thing. He really meant it this time. He had vied for the spotlight in the Clooney family and now that he had a taste of what it was like on a movie set there was nothing else he wanted to do. Not even the thrill of a grand slam home run for the Cincinnati Reds could match the excitement of the movies.

George's resentment and anger towards his parents shouldn't be construed as simply youthful pique. He was genuinely hurt and, possibly for the first time in their lives, there was a serious rift between father and son. 'It was a bad scene when I left,' said Clooney a few years later in one of his first major interviews.

Laura Laycock, as a neighbour and friend of the Clooneys, was party to all of this. George's ambition came as no real surprise to her, but she could also sympathise with his father's position. 'George would always make jokes about being an actor when we were young but it wasn't until he went to college that he really made up his mind and got serious about it,' she recalls. 'Then one day he just took off and told his family he was going to California. His dad wasn't really happy and you can't blame him really when his son was taking off with no money and no prospects. Of course,' she adds wryly, 'he's had to eat his words since then.'

Nick Clooney felt that his son showed some promise as a newscaster and wanted him to stay in Kentucky and try his hand with *PM Magazine* or some other show. What George may not have been aware of, and even if he was he would still probably have paid as much attention as most men of his age pay to their fathers, was that Nick Clooney knew whereof he spoke. In 1958 he too had tried to make it in Los Angeles. He went out there with stars in his eyes and came back with his tail between his legs. There was simply too much rejection for him to take. Although he had become successful in his own terms since then it was not the life he had foreseen for himself. He wasn't trying to limit his son's ambition, he was simply trying to protect him from the cruelty and capriciousness which he himself had suffered.

George Clooney was determined to be an actor and that meant he was determined to go to Los Angeles. He had hoped that his parents might have helped bankroll him but since that was out of the question he knew he would have to fund the trip for himself. Clooney spent the summer of 1982 doing whatever work he could to raise the money. 'I did all sorts of jobs. I did everything,' he remembers. 'I sold ladies' shoes – there's a fun job. There were all these women trying to squeeze size eight feet into size five shoes and yelling "But it should fit." I cut tobacco for a living for a long time,' he recalls. In fact after a brief career as a failed shoe salesman Clooney spent most of a broiling mid-Western summer cutting tobacco. 'That's why I don't care about working seven days a week now,' he continues. 'That's nothing. Cut tobacco for a while in the middle of August. Now that's a fun job.'

After several months of back-breaking work George Clooney felt he finally had enough to fund the trip. He said goodbye to his parents, packed his few belongings into a battered old maroon 1976 Ford Monte Carlo and headed for Hollywood. The car had been bought with some of the money he had earned over the summer. It was nicknamed 'The Danger Car' and with good reason – it seemed to be only the rust patches that were holding it together. Nonetheless it lasted the trip as he drove across country from the mid-West to California.

George Clooney had a car, his looks and 300 dollars when he left home. What he didn't have was the first clue about breaking into show business, but at least he had a better entrée than most in the shape of Aunt Rosemary and his cousin Miguel. When he got to Los Angeles he headed straight for their home in Beverly Hills. However, he didn't quite find the warm welcome that he might have expected. Rosemary Clooney was recovering from years in hospitals and years of neglect of her children. Now that she was back to full health she was determined to make up for that lost time with her own five children. She wasn't too keen on extending her emotional support network to include a wilful nephew who was out here against his parents' wishes.

In addition Rosemary, who was now even closer to Nick following the death of their sister Betty, agreed completely with her brother's assessment of George's chances in Hollywood. 'I think acting is the most thankless profession in the world,' she said recently. 'I don't think there was a finer actor than José Ferrer and I know the number of times he was rejected.'

Nonetheless, whether she agreed with him or not, the boy was family and she took him in. George stayed with his aunt for several months but it does not appear to have been a very happy experience for either of them. The arrangement was that he was going to earn his keep by acting as an unpaid handyman and doing all sorts of odd jobs around the house and the grounds. His approach to his duties was less than wholehearted. On one occasion he was asked to paint the fence around the swimming pool, the same pool presumably he had so admired and coveted on previous visits. George did what he was asked, but only up to a point. His painting extended only to that part of the fence which his aunt could see from her bedroom window, the rest was left as it was. It was a farcical scenario, reminiscent of Tom Sawyer's attempt at whitewashing his Aunt Polly's fence. Clooney didn't quite charge the neighbourhood kids to come and paint it but he might as well have done for all the use he was.

Rosemary Clooney was becoming concerned about her nephew. It wasn't just that he wasn't doing much around the house during the day, it was the fact that he seemed to spend every night out on the town with his cousins. Bearing in mind the family predisposition to drinking, and her own recent traumas, it's no wonder she was becoming worried. 'He ran pretty wild,' she says of her nephew. 'I was on the road a lot but I noticed a lot of dark circles under his eyes. I thought he was awful young for that.'

Perhaps because of that Rosemary decided it was time she kept an eye on young George herself. Her career was picking up, her voice – although never what it had been – was still in good shape, and she was in demand on tour. She decided that since George loved to drive she would take him with her on the road. He would be the driver on a tour she was booked on. Rosemary Clooney and fellow Hollywood and Broadway stars Martha Raye, Helen O'Connell and Margaret Whiting were touring through the West in a show called 4 Girls 4. The tour was an education for George, who found out a lot about life on the road. On one occasion he even found himself searching for the dentures of a movie legend – he refuses to name her out of gallantry – who, the worse for drink, had conned a lift with him and then passed out back at his place. The false teeth were eventually found in a fruit basket.

The hours were long and the bonuses few as Clooney ferried his aunt and her cronies from gig to gig. Obviously he was not happy and his resentment must have been starting to show. His aunt for her part was beginning, more and more, to treat him as much like the hired help as a member of the family. So instead of seeking fame and fortune George Clooney now found himself living a real-life Cinderella story, as the poor relation from the country living with the rich folks in Beverly Hills. Clooney claims that although his aunt was kindness itself to her own children, she was less than charitable to him. He also claims that through time that attitude spread to her children and the cousins who had been keen to party with him to begin with wanted less and less to do with him.

'I will never really be over the sense of how humiliated I was at that time,' he told an interviewer some years later. 'Humiliated in the sense that we would all be sitting around in the living room and they'd say "Okay, let's all go to dinner. George you stay here."'

To be fair to Rosemary Clooney, her nephew must have been far from sparkling company at this stage. He was doing the rounds of auditions and casting calls but getting absolutely nowhere. He had next to no money, no Screen Actors Guild union card, and no experience – being an extra in a mini-series and a walk-on part in a film which no one had ever seen cut surprisingly little ice with casting directors and agents. And if he thought that being the son of a local celebrity and the nephew of a woman whose best days were behind her was going to help him find work, he was quickly disabused of the notion. 'The truth is that casting directors don't care who Rosemary Clooney's nephew is,' he said some years later once the work had finally started to come in. 'Once I had got the job it was something to talk about, but it has nothing to do with getting a job. For the most part, people don't really give a damn who's in my family.'

The work simply was not coming in and George was becoming more and more broody and introspective. Eventually Rosemary Clooney couldn't take it any more and after a few months she simply asked her melancholy nephew to leave.

Clooney wasn't exactly homeless but it was a major setback and a severe knock to his self-confidence. He had made some friends in his round of the cattle calls by which unknown young actors try to get their foot in the Hollywood door. One of them was Tom Matthews, who was fortunate enough to be working at that time. He was also fortunate enough to have an apartment which had a large walk-in cupboard. Clooney prevailed upon him to let him live in the cupboard, which was large enough to sleep in. So, for eight months Clooney slept in Tom Matthews' cupboard. It was a kindness from a friend to a struggling newcomer which he would not forget and he and Matthews have become close friends and confidants since then. Some years later, when he had finally made the big time, Clooney would take the opportunity to return the favour to Matthews.

Tom Matthews was astounded that Clooney was able to live in the cupboard. He says he was even more astounded that the actor managed to persuade girls to come back into the closet with him. Plainly if his career was failing Clooney's charm was not and he was proving as popular with the girls in Hollywood as he had been in Augusta.

With no money coming in Clooney was once again forced to take a series of menial jobs, doing anything he could do to keep body and soul together between auditions. He was an unsuccessful insurance salesman, he was also an unsuccessful menswear salesman. His attempts to sell men's suits met with much the same result as his attempts at selling women's shoes. He also put his talent as an artist to some use by working as a caricaturist in a shopping mall. But mostly he worked in the construction industry. A couple of months in the tobacco fields meant that Clooney was no stranger to hard work and he frequently found himself moving from contract to contract. Clooney would mainly do unskilled work, mostly shovelling sand to allow the tradesmen to get on with the real construction work.

Although he and his father had not parted on the best of terms his father admired Clooney's drive and refusal to give up. This stubbornness and perseverance was almost a family trait and Nick Clooney respected his son for it. 'George showed incredible strength of character by never despairing and never complaining,' says Nick Clooney. 'Nina and I hinted that he was more than welcome to come home or turn to us but he never did. In fact, after a few years George was taking in other struggling actors and helping them out.'

George Clooney did manage to find the odd piece of acting work in that first year in Hollywood. Despite what was happening outside his career he still, by all accounts, walked into auditions brimming with self-confidence. By the time Clooney walked into a room he gave the impression that everyone else might as well go home because the job was his. Unfortunately casting directors tended not to see it that way, but now and again one of them would.

His first professional job was in a commercial for Japanese stereos. Clooney believes to this day that he got the job simply because he walked into the audition with a six-pack of cold Japanese Sapporo beer and asked if anyone fancied a drink.

Although he had found his first job what he really needed was continuity of employment. It wasn't enough to do the occasional commercial and then head back to the building site. Man cannot live by stereo commercials alone, he needs steady work. Once again, as it had been back in Lexington, it was cousin Miguel who came up with the solution.

Chapter 7:
ER – The First
Time

Although his cousin had not necessarily endeared himself to the rest of the household, Miguel Ferrer remained fond of George Clooney. He remembered the times they had spent together hanging out and having fun down in Lexington. Perhaps he also felt a sense of obligation. It was Ferrer who, after all, had got George into this position. It was Ferrer who had called him and told him to come to Lexington and hang out while they shot the movie.

Whatever the reasons, Miguel Ferrer knew even better than George Clooney that there was a world of difference between getting work and having a career. What George really needed was an agent but he was unlikely to get an agent without having any credits to his name. Of course, in the perennial Catch-22 situation, the chances of getting those credits without an agent were next to impossible. There were only so many jobs available that could be got from open casting calls, anything decent needed the recommendation of a respected agent.

The first step to getting an agent was by impressing him with your résumé. George Clooney's résumé – a Japanese stereo commercial, a film that was never released, and a face in the crowd in a mini-series – would not rate so much as a passing glance from a halfway decent agent. The answer was, with a little help from Miguel, to make the résumé a little more interesting. 'I had to make kind of a phoney résumé at first,' Clooney admits. 'I lied about a lot of regional theatre things that I couldn't get caught for, and I made myself very familiar with the plays I had said I'd been in in case I was ever asked.'

This isn't actually lying, or at least it isn't lying in actors' terms. Actors are frequently economical with the truth provided it helps them get a job. If you're an actor and they ask if you can ride a horse or a unicycle or sky dive, then the only acceptable response is emphatically in the affirmative. If you get the job then it's up to you to acquire some equestrian skills pretty smartly. So all that Clooney was doing with his fake résumé was the equivalent of admitting he could ride a horse.

Fortunately for him Clooney was never called on his résumé. His natural good looks and his self-confidence – genuine or otherwise – were generally enough to get him through the front door. Eventually he found an agent but ironically the fake résumé didn't play any part in the process. He was recommended to his first representatives through a friend of a friend.

The one other factor which it is important to remember at this stage was that, no matter how handsome he was – and he was maturing into pin-up boy good looks – Clooney couldn't act to save his life at this stage. Even now he will self-deprecatingly play down his talents as an actor. But back in 1982 he was barely able to move round the set without bumping into the furniture. Certainly he had appeared in *Fiddler on the Roof* back at Beef and Boards and he had performed on his father's show, but that hardly counted as acting. What he had been doing was larking about and having fun.

To his credit Clooney knew then, as he does now, the extent of his limitations. He never put himself up to play Hamlet, for example. But he did know that it was important to bring himself up to speed as quickly as possible on the rudiments of stage craft, voice control and all the other weapons in the professional actor's arsenal.

Clooney was assiduously going to acting classes. He was learning in Los Angeles from Milton Katselas, a highly-respected tutor. In fact, Clooney was so inexperienced that his classes began with one of Katselas's assistants before being taught by Katselas himself. It was a revelation to Clooney. 'Class made a big difference,' he says. 'If you want to be around a very positive place and be involved in something that really pushes you to work, Milton's class does that. The whole thing is confidence.'

The discipline of acting class certainly changed George Clooney. For the past few years he had been wandering aimlessly and without any real direction. Even when he found something that he thought he wanted to do with his life in the shape of acting, he wasn't really applying himself. Milton Katselas challenged Clooney. If Clooney was going to be an actor then he would have to apply the same sort of concentration and direction he would have applied with the Cincinnati Reds. If he wanted to be an actor then he was going to have to step up to the plate and swing at it.

Clooney responded to the challenge. He applied himself and he started to improve dramatically to the point where he was able to take part in one of Katselas's showcase productions. These productions were very well-respected and attracted representatives from all the major agencies who were there to check on new talent. George Clooney had two lines in one of these productions but at the end of the show he had a new agent.

The change of agency certainly started things happening for Clooney. He found himself going out for more and more jobs. There were fewer cattle calls, now at least he was going with an appointment. But still the auditions weren't turning into much in the way of regular employment.

Once again Miguel offered some valuable advice. He reminded George of his father and Uncle George. He reminded him of how easy-going and relaxed they both were, especially when they were dealt seconds in the great game of life. In short, he told George to relax and lighten up. It may have been the best piece of advice anyone had ever given him. It doesn't do for George Clooney to be too serious, he is at his best when he's out there flying and taking chances. He had done live television, he could work an audience, he knew exactly how far he could go and he started to apply that to his auditions. 'I think I'm good at comedy but I'm smarter at taking chances,' he remembers.

There was an audition when Clooney was up for the part of the lead singer in a punk rock band. It's hard to imagine anyone less in the image of a punk than the classically handsome Clooney. Nonetheless, there he was in torn T-shirt, spiky hair and ripped jeans giving it his best shot. When he came to the part of the script where the band's name was mentioned for the first time Clooney stunned everyone by tearing off his T-shirt completely to reveal the name of the band – Body Fluids – tattooed on his chest. The tattoo was only temporary of course but it served its purpose.

'They told me later that's what got me the job,' says Clooney. 'I don't know how I came up with that. You just kind of do it with whatever is lying around. If the material itself isn't very funny then you do something with it. Class taught me that. You don't have to do what the sides say. If you do the obvious people don't react.'

George Clooney had done the unexpected and it had paid off – he had the job. He also had the confidence to do whatever he felt he had to in an audition to show them his stuff. Slowly but surely the work started to arrive.

In 1983 he made his first real movie. It was a low budget film, just as *And They're Off* had been, but this time it had some kind of pedigree and – more importantly for Clooney – some dialogue. There is a great deal of confusion over Clooney's first movie. It is frequently reported that he had a part in the Arnold Schwarzenegger film *Predator*. This John McTiernan-directed action vehicle was the movie which, probably more than anything else, made Schwarzenegger an international star. However, it could not have done the same for George Clooney because he wasn't in the 1987 movie. By 1987 indeed Clooney was well established on American television with a face which was every bit as well-known as Arnold Schwarzenegger's.

In fact George Clooney's first "real" movie role came in the 1983 film *Grizzly II – The Predator*. The original *Grizzly*, about a man-eating bear on the rampage, had been made in 1976 to cash in on the phenomenal success of *Jaws*. The poster in fact carried the advertising copyline 'Claws'. Now some seven years later they were making a sequel. The growth of the video market in the intervening period meant that a cheaply-made sequel could easily turn a profit on video. So George Clooney found himself starring in a movie with Charlie Sheen and Laura Dern. Of the three of them only Dern had acted in a movie before, Sheen and Clooney were both making their screen debuts.

Grizzly II – The Predator was not a success. In fact it was never released. For Clooney all he got out of it in material terms was a small fee and some more experience. However, the shared experience of making a cheap, bad film in straitened circumstances did leave him with an abiding friendship with both Laura Dern and Charlie Sheen.

Grizzly II was very definitely a 'B' movie but it was work. And there was more on the way. In the same year as his abortive movie debut Clooney got his first real television job. His flair for comedy landed him a part in a sitcom which was to star Elliot Gould and Jason Alexander, later to become a household name as George in *Seinfeld*.

Gould – who was once married to Barbra Streisand – had been a major star in the Seventies; he had starred in *M.A.S.H.*, *The Long Goodbye*, *California Split* and *Nashville*. In one of his early movies, the controversially trendy *Bob & Carol & Ted & Alice*, he had been nominated for a Best Supporting Actor Oscar.

His best movie work was behind him by the early Eighties and he was ready to try the first of what eventually amounted to three situation comedies. Clooney had a regular part in the first of them. The show was called *Emergency Room*, but was more commonly referred to simply as *E.R.*. The coincidence between the title of his first show and the show which would make him a household name is almost unnerving. So too is the fact that it was set in the emergency room of a Chicago hospital.

Unfortunately for George Clooney, who played Ace, the smart-talking intern, the similarity between the two shows extends only to the titles. While the current dramatic version of *ER* conquers the ratings wherever it is shown, the Elliott Gould version was a dismal failure. After only eight weeks on air the show was cancelled.

'The "young hunk" thing is why he was cast on my *E.R.*,' says Elliott Gould. 'But he was playing a boy, a very young man. In the new *ER* he seems to have matured and really come into his own."'

Clooney wasn't too downhearted by the cancellation of *Emergency Room*. He had got the part after all, he had worked for a couple of months and he had picked up more valuable experience. But more importantly for him, he could not be tainted by the failure of the show. It wasn't his fault that the series flopped, so he could simply dust himself down and start looking for something else.

A short time later Clooney had another real shot at some halfway decent work when he got an audition with John Crosby at the giant ABC television network. Crosby was vice-president of casting at that time and if Clooney could impress him then he would be taking a major step up the ladder. His audition was supposed to be a brief solo scene with no props. However, the scene that Clooney had chosen, a key moment from Neil Simon's autobiographical comedy *Brighton Beach Memoirs*, required two actors, each in the upper and lower tiers of a bunk bed.

Clooney came into the audition, composed himself, and then shouted 'Okay, let's do it.' On his command five burly friends each wearing a T-shirt with the word 'Roadie' on the back came into the room carrying pieces of bunk bed. 'They came in and snapped those beds together in no time,' Clooney recalls. 'Then a friend of mine, Grant Heslove, and I did the scene from *Brighton Beach Memoirs*. It was supposed to be a three minute scene with no props, we did fifteen minutes in bunk beds. It doesn't mean you have to be obnoxious to get their attention. It means you have to know how to pull it off. I just took a shot, but I don't take giant risks. It was pretty calculated,' says Clooney, tacitly conceding that the bunk beds could have been broken down just as quickly by security guards and he could have been out on his ear with no chance of ever working at ABC.

'The secretary was going crazy and yelling "You can't do this, you can't do this",' he remembers. 'But I just told her "Don't worry. We can pull this off." And John Crosby loved it.'

Crosby did indeed love it. He loved it so much that Clooney left the audition with a four-month contract with ABC which would lead to his first genuine television role. But Crosby wasn't silly. No one hands out contracts in Hollywood just because they are amused by the unconventional. Crosby gave Clooney a contract because of his acting ability, not his carpentry skills.

For the first time in his life George Clooney had steady work. Crosby had placed him under a four-month contract and it was that contract that really got the ball rolling. Clooney grew in confidence and became more and more ambitious, especially in his stage work. In Los Angeles he started doing more and more theatre work, usually in Equity-waiver productions. This meant that he didn't need an Equity card but on the other hand he would be working for next to nothing. But he was getting good notices and before too long he found himself at the Steppenwolf Theatre in Chicago, playing a drug dealer in *Vicious*, a play about Sex Pistols member and punk icon Sid Vicious. The Steppenwolf Theatre is one of America's most prestigious theatrical venues. It is the home of the Steppenwolf Company, whose founders and prominent members include Gary Sinise, John Malkovich and Laurie Metcalf. In theatrical terms Clooney was in the big leagues and he was starting to attract attention.

'It's the only play I've done that was really worth seeing,' said Clooney of *Vicious* in a 1985 interview. '*Vicious* was dirty and it was nasty, but there was a certain energy about it and it was chic so everybody was coming to see it.'

At the age of 23 George Clooney was finally coming to believe that he could make something of himself at the acting business after all.

Chapter 8:
Learning the
Facts of Life

L ife was changing for George Clooney and changing fast. He had arrived in Hollywood at the age of 21 with nothing to speak of except his looks, his confidence and his self-belief. Two years later things were happening.

The Danger Car – that old 76 Monte Carlo – had long gone. It had got him from Augusta to Beverly Hills and just about expired in the process. His car of choice at the moment was a thing of beauty, a 1960 Oldsmobile convertible Dynamic 88. Cars mean a lot to Clooney and always have done. When he would finally make the big time, he would use his car as the one place where he could not be bothered. He would drive around in his car learning his lines. 'Driving for me is therapy,' he says. 'That's my one place where I won't be hassled. You kind of need to get away from people telling you how good things are. You've got to get by yourself and say "All right now, what is this? What's this really amounting to?"'

Clooney had found the vintage Oldsmobile and added his own little touches, like new carpeting throughout. And to add that final touch of retro chic, Clooney even had fluffy dice hanging from the rear view mirror. 'I work on it all the time, every other day,' said Clooney of the real love of his life. 'It's a really classic car, great lines, and really long. I get two tickets when I park it in a car park,' he joked. 'It's art on wheels.'

And who cares if the dice looked naff, Clooney was one of the hottest and best-looking young talents in town. At least that's what people kept telling him. 'It's very easy to sit in a room when you're 23 and have every-one go "Hey, you're the greatest", and believe it,' says Clooney. 'Which I think I did for a minute, to be honest, because I think I had good TV hair.'

Clooney did once, self-deprecatingly, call himself 'a hair actor and proud of it', a reference to the way he was tending to be cast as cookie-cutter characters with only the hairstyles altered to tell them apart.

It's not surprising that Clooney believed people, no matter how briefly, when they told him he was the greatest. Hadn't he been telling people the same for years? Isn't that what his boisterous boasting to his teacher Bill Case really amounted to back in his final year of high school? But there must surely have been an element of bravado in all of his proud claims. Clooney knew first hand from his father about the pain of rejection, and he only had to look at his Aunt Rosemary's career to see how briefly the flame of showbiz celebrity could be dimmed.

'She unfortunately believed people when they told her "You are a goddess",' says Clooney of his famous aunt. 'So when that got taken away and those same people told her "It's your fault", she believed that too. That destroyed her. It took her a while to get back on her feet.'

But the one thing which kept George Clooney rooted in reality, or as close to reality as an actor gets, was his father. Although there had been something of a schism when Clooney left for Hollywood, no one should underestimate the effect that his father has had on George Clooney's career. The two men are close now. Nick Clooney is inordinately proud of his son to the point where he accosted complete strangers in an Australian airport to point out his son on the cover of *Newsweek*. George Clooney has reached that stage in life that all men reach where he has realised that maybe he didn't know as much as he thought he did. And maybe his father knew more than he credited him with.

'My dad was probably the best for me about understanding the basic law of show business which is that you are never as bad as they say you are when you're bad,' says Clooney, 'and you're never as good as you are when they say you're good.

'Once you understand that,' he concludes, 'you'll survive anything.'

His father's advice kept Clooney level-headed at a very appropriate period in his life. By 1985, at the age of 24, he was becoming a face. He was one of those people who television audiences vaguely recognised without yet being able to put a name to. He had reached the 'Isn't that whatsisname?' stage of an actor's career.

His brief stint in Elliott Gould's *Emergency Room* had started it, but then came a higher-profile role which would build on that. Following on from that chaotic but successful reading of *Brighton Beach Memoirs* for John Crosby, Clooney landed a regular role in *The Facts of Life*, a popular NBC family-oriented comedy. He played George Burnett, a carpenter and handy-man. 'In *Emergency Room* I played Conchata Ferrell's nephew and I was just a screw up,' says Clooney of the range of parts he was getting. 'In *Facts of Life* I'm just the guy who comes in and hassles people and leaves. It's more what I can do with comedy that got me the jobs.'

No matter how he got the jobs, the fact that he was getting them at all was big news back in Augusta. His father had pulled in 60 and 70 ratings shares in his heyday but there was nothing to compare with the numbers George pulled down when he made his first appearance in *The Facts of Life*. Every television set in Augusta was tuned to NBC the night George made his debut.

'That really was the first thing I remember seeing him in,' says Laura Laycock. 'It was a big event in Augusta. I was very happy for him, I think everybody was. But I remember that it didn't seem like George. I don't know who I thought it was but it just didn't seem like our George,' she says. 'But that was the start of things for him and we were all very proud of him.'

Clooney was also gaining a reputation as a pin-up. Publicity material from the period went out of its way to describe him as a heartthrob. Even from the earliest interviews Clooney has always played down the glamour boy tag, even though he admits it is better than being thought of as the ugly one. But he conceded that his naturally telegenic looks had played their part. 'I don't think my looks hurt me,' he said in an early interview. 'But the parts I go up for aren't specifically the good-looking guy parts,' he insisted. 'They're just the guy parts.'

Although Clooney was doing well by 1984 when he became a regular on *The Facts of Life* and making decent money for the first time in his life, he was still not the master of his fate. He was at that stage in an actor's life where the work was choosing him rather than the other way around. It would take another ten years before that magical transformation would take place. And Clooney was smart enough to know that, in Hollywood terms, he was just another good-looking boy – no matter how hot.

The one place where Clooney was able to choose the work was on stage. He had an element of financial security now and that gave him a certain freedom in his experimental stage work. 'I really enjoy doing comedy and I enjoy the fact that I have the money to do things I really want to do,' Clooney said in a 1985 interview, not long after he became a regular on *The Facts of Life*. 'I'm in the process of buying a play now and I'll be able to produce theatre. Theatre is where you learn everything. You learn how to make characters interesting because you die if you don't. I mean you die and you know you're dying because you're in front of everybody,' he said. 'I like the feeling of an audience.'

Given his love of cars it's not surprising that George Clooney named his production company Dynamic 88, after his beloved Oldsmobile. To his credit, while his production company was getting off the ground, Clooney was continuing to spend time honing his craft and learning as much as he could about acting. In December 1985, he and Miguel Ferrer teamed up on stage in Los Angeles. It was the first time they had acted together since the abortive *And They're Off*.

It was Ferrer who had come up with the idea of doing the play *Wrestlers*, a two-hander which he had seen at the Cast Theatre in Los Angeles in the summer of 1985. The play was written by Bill Davis, who was starring in it along with Mark Harmon. By one of those odd quirks of show-biz fate Harmon, like Clooney, was another actor who would become a big name in a TV medical show – in his case *St Elsewhere* – while at the same time struggling to have his ability as an actor seen above his leading man good looks. Ferrer had liked the play and wanted to do it with his friend Shaun Cassidy.

Cassidy, like Ferrer and Clooney, was the product of a show-business family. He was the son of Jack Cassidy and MGM musical star Shirley Jones, and he was the younger brother of Seventies teen idol David Cassidy. Shaun had been a teen idol himself briefly when he starred with Parker Stevenson in television's *The Hardy Boys*. Cassidy has now given up acting and enjoys a successful career as a writer and producer, most notably of the horror series *American Gothic*.

Despite Ferrer's insistence that it would be the perfect vehicle for both of them, Cassidy was busy with other things by the end of 1985 and couldn't do it. When Ferrer mentioned this to his cousin, Clooney suggested that they do it instead. Ferrer quickly warmed to the idea and the two of them worked on some scenes together to convince the show's backers that they could carry it off. It wasn't as simple as it appeared on the surface. 'The producers wanted to know we had enough draw to get an audience in,' says an incredulous Clooney.

Bearing in mind that Clooney was featured in one of the country's top television shows and that this was an Equity-waiver production in a small theatre, one assumes enough people would come along out of sheer curiosity to fill the hall. Nonetheless the producers were insistent. To satisfy them Clooney got his publicist to send them a press pack which kept them happy. However there was still a problem over Miguel Ferrer. Again Clooney solved that one by helping his cousin 'create' a biography, presumably in the same way that Ferrer had created a résumé for Clooney a couple of years previously.

Eventually the producers were convinced and gave their permission just three weeks before *Wrestlers* opened at the Cast Theatre in December 1985.

'It's a fun show to do but I was a nervous wreck the first night,' said Clooney in an interview during the play's limited engagement. 'Three weeks ago they told us we had got it, then it took a week for them to get us a revised script. Then things came up around Thanksgiving so we had to open a week earlier than we had thought. 'There's no time to stop and breathe during this show, I tell you, it is the worst feeling to be thinking "I don't know if I'm going to remember my lines." But I love being this busy. I'm either really working and have no time at all or I have so much spare time because unlike other actors I can't go on interviews. I've got a job. And when I'm working I go nuts,' he added in mock exasperation, 'because there is no time to get to all those stupid, regular things you have to do between nine and five.'

By the end of 1985, with the run of *Wrestlers* completed, George Clooney was in a reflective mood. He had come a significant way in a very short time. There were others – and many of them would be more talented – who would struggle all their lives and not achieve a fraction of what he had done in three years. George Clooney was the last person who needed to be told that, but he still allowed himself a measure of self-congratulation. 'Sometimes,' he said in that same 1985 interview, 'I'll wake up and think "I'm very happy that I decided to do this." I mean,' he continues, 'I wasn't married. I didn't have any kids. Everyone said I was really stupid to come out here. 'But I'm really happy I did because I would have spent the rest of my life in Cincinnati wishing I had come out here.'

Chapter 9:
Roseanne

There comes a moment in every successful actor's life when fate or luck or whatever else you care to call it finally decides to take a hand. It's the 'big break'; that magic moment when your career will never be the same again.

For different actors the big break comes in different ways. For Robert De Niro it was meeting Martin Scorsese at a Christmas party and taking the first steps towards forming the greatest creative collaboration in American cinema. For Sharon Stone it was having the guts to leave her underwear at home for *Basic Instinct* and ending years of struggling in 'B' movie roles. More recently for Nicolas Cage, it was the double-whammy of appearing in *Leaving Las Vegas* and *The Rock* within months of each other, telling Hollywood he could act – *Leaving Las Vegas* won him an Oscar – and carry a $100 million grossing action film.

For George Clooney, the big break was just around the corner as he went into 1986. The stage career which he had eagerly talked about never materialised. It wasn't that he lost interest in buying and producing plays with his new-found wealth, it was just that he simply didn't have the time. *Wrestlers* would be George Clooney's last stage appearance because his television career was about to take off.

There was one more disappointment along the way, however. During the run of *Wrestlers* George was growing his hair long for a new ABC cop series called *Sunset Beat*. Clooney was playing a character called, improbably enough, Chic Chesboro in this allegedly hip crime show. *Sunset Beat* was a disaster and had one of the shortest runs in television history. It was cancelled after only two shows.

After some of the praise which had been lavished on him, Clooney might have been entitled to feel despondent about the dismal failure of *Sunset Beat*. But his father's advice about never being as good or as bad as they say you are stood him in good stead. So too, and not for the first time, did the small-town values of hard work and perseverance which had been engrained in him. After *Sunset Beat* flopped Clooney just got on with his career.

He had money in the bank, there were jobs in the pipeline and he was making friends in high places. George Clooney was getting noticed both by Warners and NBC. Both companies were delighted to bide their time in the sure and certain knowledge that George Clooney was going to be a major television star. 'George Clooney's greatest asset is his great ass. We noticed it first on *The Facts of Life*,' said Warren Littlefield famously and memorably. Littlefield is the president of the entertainment division of NBC, the network for which Clooney and his colleagues delivers millions of viewers on a weekly basis in *ER*.

Clooney's reaction to the comment are not recorded but they must at least have been ambivalent. He was an actor after all and no actor wants to be remembered for parts of their anatomy rather than the parts they play. On the other hand he would be sanguine enough to realise that if a great ass was what it took to get regular work, then thank God he had a great ass. Great screen actors like Paul Newman, Clint Eastwood and Robert Redford had all been cast for their looks in the early part of their career. If Clooney was to be cast for his looks then it would be up to him to do something with the work. He already believed that, although his looks had got him the parts in *Emergency Room* and *The Facts of Life*, it was his skill with comedy which had kept him there. He would simply have to accept the fact that his looks would open the door and he could then go on and prove his talent.

In 1988 the ABC network was putting together a comedy series which would be a vehicle for a former waitress from Denver who had become a sensation on the stand-up circuit. The waitress-turned-comedienne was Roseanne Barr and a series of high-rating and well-received comedy specials on the HBO cable channel had convinced the powers that be at ABC that she could handle a sitcom. It turned out to be one of the smartest moves ABC ever made because *Roseanne*, as the show was called, became a ratings blockbuster. It was, and remains, one of the most popular shows on television all over the world, either in first-run or syndication. It established Barr – she would change her name to Roseanne Arnold two years later when she married comedian Tom Arnold – as the most powerful woman in television. Indeed, as *Roseanne* continued its staggeringly successful run, she would become the most powerful and influential woman in television since Lucille Ball.

Like Ball before her, Roseanne Barr's television persona was an extension of her own life. It was impossible on *I Love Lucy* or *The Lucy Show* to tell where Lucille Ball stopped and Lucille McGillicuddy or Lucy Carmichael began. The line between Roseanne Barr and her fictional creation Roseanne Connor – the show is described simply as 'based on a character created by Roseanne Barr' – is similarly blurred.

Roseanne Connor was a blue-collar mother of three struggling to get by. She worked in a plastics factory, husband Dan was a small-time building contractor. Money was tight for the Connors and if the American Dream hadn't exactly stiffed them they were entitled to feel they had been at the very least short-changed. But audiences loved Roseanne and her mordant view of blue-collar life in the reality of a post-Reaganomics economy. This was a view of American life a million miles away from *Leave it to Beaver* and *Father Knows Best*. There were no easy answers and the audience ate it up because they recognised themselves in the Connors.

Again like Lucille Ball, Barr had an enormous input into the production. She surrounded herself with a superb ensemble cast led by John Goodman as her husband and Steppenwolf Theatre veteran Laurie Metcalf as her sister.

Roseanne was a hot show and despite its star vehicle status it had a large ensemble cast of family, friends and workmates for Barr's character. The buzz around the television sector of Hollywood was that George Clooney was a hot property. *Roseanne* seemed like the ideal place for ABC to cast him. Clooney appeared in the first season of the show as Booker, the male-chauvinist, blue-collar department head in the plastics factory where Roseanne works. Almost instantly George Clooney found himself, for the first time in his life, with a role in the country's most-watched television show. But it all happened by mistake.

'I actually read for the wrong part,' he reveals. He had gone along for one of the other roles but they gave him the Booker script by accident. 'But I ended up getting the job because I was funny.'

It was the big break. He had gone from being 'whatsisname' to 'that guy from *Roseanne*' and he was making more money than he had ever seen in his life. But however he had imagined his success, it couldn't have been quite like this. Even though he was now rich and moderately famous there were still major problems. Not least because although he had the part, there was a strong suspicion that he may not actually have been right for it.

Booker was supposed to be a nasty piece of work. He was Roseanne's nemesis, he was the bane of her working life, he was the bad guy she could bitch to Dan about. But the very qualities which were finally making Clooney a success in his career were working against him here. Put simply, Clooney was just too cute to be nasty. No matter how hard he tried to be an ogre he just never looked convincing. And it was a problem that people were becoming aware of.

'I heard people talking about that all the time,' recalled Sara Gilbert, who played Roseanne's screen daughter Darleen, in a *TV Guide* interview at the time. 'It was always a real challenge to make him seem unlikeable.'

Clooney too was aware of the problem. Perhaps because he knew that he really wasn't right for the part he felt that his jokes weren't coming off. And for a man who had prided himself on his ability to play comedy, and had got the part because he was so funny at the reading, that must have been a very unnerving situation. No matter what kind of doubts he may have had, however, Clooney continued to turn in thoroughly professional performances. He also began to indulge his penchant for practical jokes. Clooney had been a prankster since his high school days and now any set he is working on is fair game for his tricks, but on Roseanne it was a little bit of a first.

'He always has something funny to say,' said Gilbert in that *TV Guide* interview of her co-star. 'He'll pretend to vomit up food or dislocate his neck or do anything revolting. But he can pull it off because he is so charming all the while,' she insisted. 'I think he's really attractive, but his attraction comes out of his sense of humour and his personality as much as it does out of the aesthetics of George.'

Practical jokes on a TV or movie set can be something of a mixed blessing. At best they can defuse tension and lighten the situation, at worst they can be time-consuming and cause expensive re-shoots. On that first season of *Roseanne*, however, Clooney's pranks and gags were welcome to lighten up an atmosphere that could easily tend towards the poisonous.

Clooney looks back on his year on the show as a difficult one for him, partly because of the on-set problems. There were frequent fights and arguments, although fortunately none of them involved him. Roseanne Barr had created the show and quite properly wanted to protect her vision of her character and the environment in which she operated. On the other hand, executive producer Matt Williams had a duty to the network to bring the show in on time and on budget. There were a lot of on-set and behind the scenes arguments between Barr and Williams which ultimately had an effect on the rest of the cast. 'It was very volatile,' says Clooney looking back on his stint on *Roseanne*.

However, Clooney himself was anointed. *Roseanne* really showcased his romantic potential to a nationwide audience for the first time. If he could emerge as attractive and loveable even while playing the heavy then that said something about his future career direction. Co-star Sara Gilbert described Clooney as 'a dreamboat'. Roseanne Barr was also an admirer. Whether she thought Clooney was a dreamboat or not, she respected him for his professionalism and his craft. She also admired the way that Clooney was prepared to stand up for himself and give as good as he got, even when she was the one on the other side of the discussion.

The feeling was mutual and Clooney is full of admiration for Roseanne the woman, if not his experience on *Roseanne* the show. 'She was hysterical,' he says with genuine fondness. 'She was the foulest woman I ever met and I thought I was foul,' he adds with admiration. Roseanne doubtless would take that as a heartfelt compliment.

Although he was popular with Roseanne Barr and the rest of the cast and the network loved him, Clooney as Booker was still something of a problem. Everyone suspected that the character didn't really fit in, but no one wanted to lose an actor of Clooney's quality and appeal. There was talk of a spin-off.

One idea, suggested not entirely in jest by John Goodman, was that *Roseanne* might provide a launch-pad for another series starring Clooney and Laurie Metcalf. Goodman bandied about the notion that Booker and Roseanne's sister might end up getting married and spinning off into a show of their own with the impetus of *Roseanne's* first season blockbuster ratings to help them.

Deep down, though, Clooney was as dissatisfied with the situation as everyone else seemed to be satisfied with it. The big ratings and the high salary didn't matter that much to him. He described himself at the time as 'the seventh banana in the Number One show'. An accurate, albeit cynical summary of the situation, and certainly not one with which an ambitious 27-year-old would have been happy with.

So, as the first season of *Roseanne* ended, George Clooney said good-bye to a part which could have made him secure for life. He wasn't happy, he didn't feel he was giving of his best, so he quit.

Chapter 10:
A Golden Couple

George Clooney had been telling people for years that he was going to be a movie star. No one had really taken him seriously; even when he made it on the small screen those who knew him still found the situation a little unreal. But Clooney believed that he would eventually make it on the big screen.

Increasingly, though, it was harder and harder to convince himself. He had been doing television for almost five years and still the movie break hadn't materialised. *Roseanne* had made him a nationally recognised face but it didn't bring him any closer to the career he really wanted.

That wasn't for want of trying. There had been a good many attempts to break into the movies. His looks and comic timing made him a natural for the John Hughes teen comedies which did good box office in the Eighties, but he just couldn't get the parts. He had come close in 1985 to taking one of the key roles in Hughes' *The Breakfast Club*. This was a story of a group of disaffected, delinquent teenagers who reach a point of mutual understanding during a day-long detention period at school. Clooney was being considered for the role of the delinquent rebel – although at 24 he would have been a bit long in the tooth for a teenager. However, in the end he lost out to Judd Nelson. It was the first of several occasions in which Nelson would be preferred to Clooney in Hughes' pictures. Clooney may have felt aggrieved at the time but given their subsequent career paths it's unlikely now that he would want to change places with Nelson.

The Breakfast Club was a major international success and it's interesting to speculate what might have happened had Clooney been cast. Would he have faded into relative obscurity like Nelson? Or would he have stayed the course as spectacularly as, say, Tom Cruise, who had broken through two years earlier in the similarly teen-oriented *Risky Business*?

The movies would have to wait for the time being and it was back to serving his time and making big money on television for Clooney. However, he must have been almost desperate for some kind of film career. Later interviews would suggest that it was starting to get to him. How else do you explain his decision to take a role in *Return of the Killer Tomatoes* in 1988? By this stage Clooney was a TV veteran. He had a certain reputation and a certain standing within the industry. He was also making a lot of money. But he still agreed to take a one-line role in a film which could barely be described as a 'B' movie. It was all very well doing *Grizzly II – The Predator* when you were glad of the work, but you can't even begin to apply those criteria this time round.

Attack of the Killer Tomatoes was made in 1977 and is one of the great bad movies. Produced and directed by John De Bello, it was a low-budget spoof of those famous Fifties science fiction movies about killer insects, animals and just about anything they could think of. The film would have been forgotten but for the growth of the video market and the fact that 'bad films' had suddenly become fashionable. Ten years later, purely to satisfy the video market, along came *Return of the Killer Tomatoes*. *Addams Family* veteran John Astin once again took the role of mad scientist Professor Gangrene, who now plans to take over the world with his tomato warriors. The film, again produced and directed by De Bello, relied heavily on flash-backs to the first movie.

Clooney is almost unrecognisable in a part which can barely be much bigger than the one he had got by accident in *And They're Off*! Apart from Astin, the only other member of the cast who went on to achieve anything of note was Teri Weigel, who would later become famous as a porn star. Clooney's contribution to the film consists of a single line in which he is required to say – with a straight face – 'That was the bravest thing I've ever seen a vegetable do.' Clooney's much publicised sense of humour must have been on manual override for that one.

There were two further movies in the series – *Killer Tomatoes Strike Back* and *Killer Tomatoes Eat France* – but fortunately Clooney had sense enough not to get involved with either of them.

George Clooney was trapped in a gilded cage. *Roseanne* had been the big break but he had walked away from it because it wasn't what he wanted. He was now a veteran of four TV series but still hadn't found what he was looking for. The money was great but the scripts and the characters were dreadful. He seemed destined forever to be cast because he had a great ass.

Professionally things were not going well, but in his personal life things were looking up. Or at least they appeared to be.

George Clooney had never suffered from a lack of female company. Whether it was the girls who lined up to watch him walk home from Augusta High School or whether it was the women who subjected themselves to the claustrophobic confines of the walk-in cupboard in Tom Matthews' apartment, pretty girls were never far away when George was around. Clooney got work on the strength of his appeal to women who went crazy over his leading-man looks. Now, however, he was settling down.

In the old days of the studio system, movie moguls would frequently engineer romances between starlets to keep the gossip columnists and the fan press happy. Those days are gone but no studio boss could have been anything but ecstatic over George Clooney's choice of partner. By the end of 1988 Clooney had settled down and begun a live-in relationship with Kelly Preston. She was a rising movie star, he was a rising TV star, together they were two of Hollywood's beautiful people. It was a match made in tabloid heaven, and style magazines like *People* rushed to feature them in its pages.

Preston had been around Hollywood for some time and although she was a year younger than Clooney, her career to that point had been more high profile. Born in Honolulu, she had come to the mainland to study drama at University of California and UCLA in Los Angeles before breaking into the business with a recurring role in the soap opera *Capitol*. She had also starred in two unsuccessful TV series – *For Love and Honor* in 1983 and *Blue Thunder* in 1984 – before breaking into movies in 1983 with a role in *Christine*, based on the Stephen King bestseller. There were other minor roles in films like *Metalstorm* and *52 Pick Up*, but by the time she and Clooney got together she was ready to step up a gear.

She had been married to actor Kevin Gage, with whom she had starred in the family movie *Space Camp* in 1986. The following year the marriage broke up. She and Clooney shared an agent at that time and she had noticed him around the building. Eventually, as these things happen in Hollywood, it was the agent who brought them together by inviting them both to the same party. 'George gave me a ride there and I was hooked,' says Preston.

Clooney seems to have been similarly smitten in what appears to have been a whirlwind romance. Just over three weeks after they had met – 23 days to be exact – the couple had bought a $1 million home together and were preparing to move in. It was that kind of relationship, a relationship based on grand gestures. For her birthday, for example, Clooney bought her a black Vietnamese pot-bellied pig called Max. 'When I saw Max I screamed,' Preston told *People* magazine. 'I really loved him. The only thing was that Max was scared of me at first. I think it was because he was castrated by the woman who had owned him previously.'

Having gone to the trouble of buying a pig for his lady love and then having the pig not want to go near her might have put out most men. George Clooney, however, had a ready solution. The one thing the pig did love was food and he would do anything for something to eat. Clooney then took to feeding him out of Preston's clothing – her bra to be exact – to encourage a little bonding. 'He ate out of my bra to learn to love me,' Preston insists. 'After a while it worked and he did love me.'

Clooney and Preston settled down to a life of colour-supplement perfection in their Hollywood home. Preston insisted that she was 'satisfied to be home baking gingerbread and decorating'. Clooney started building his own furniture and renewing his passion for things automotive by buying and restoring old cars. Life was sweet. In career terms things could-n't be going any better. Preston had paid her dues and had now been cast in two big films. She was to play opposite Arnold Schwarzenegger and Danny De Vito in *Twins*, which would be a runaway hit, and she had also signed to star opposite John Travolta in *The Experts*.

While Clooney was filming *Roseanne*, Preston was away filming *Twins*. In this broad Ivan Reitman fantasy she plays the woman to whom the genetically perfect, test-tube man-child Arnold Schwarzenegger loses his virginity. She claimed working with Schwarzenegger was so energetic that she should have got stunt pay. The love scenes were a different story, however. 'Arnie is a terrific kisser,' Preston told reporters, 'but he's not as good as my man'.

Clooney for his part appeared to be happier than he had ever been. He would happily pose for pictures with Preston as they fed their ribbon-bedecked pig in the back yard of their home. As usual, the born prankster would make light of the situation. He claimed he was only interested in her for her money and her car – she drove a Jaguar which would, joking or not, have been a big draw to a car nut like Clooney. He also jokingly insisted that they had only ended up together because she had simply gone through their agent's client list until she had found someone she liked.

Clooney had had more than his share of girlfriends and it might seem surprising that he should fall so quickly and so spectacularly for Preston.

But then perhaps there is a strong streak of the Southern romantic in him. Perhaps they just clicked. The more likely solution is that, whether he knew it or not – and he probably did – Clooney was on the rebound.

Five years earlier, in 1984, Clooney had been in a play with actress Talia Balsam. Like him, she came from a showbiz background. Her father was the Oscar-winning actor Martin Balsam and her mother was the actress Joyce Van Patten. The two had fallen in love but with both of them trying to make their way in show business their relationship didn't prosper. Eventually they broke up but Clooney felt it particularly badly. He had been in love for the first time in his life and the break-up left him deeply scarred. It's reasonable to assume that Clooney never really got over Talia Balsam. When Kelly Preston came along he was still looking for love and she was in the right place at the right time. She too was coming out of a bad relationship at the end of her two-year marriage to Kevin Gage and they simply provided each other with some welcome solace.

In a *People* magazine article in February 1989, designed to show off their home and how much in love they were, Clooney and Preston spoke of their future plans together. The two of them, according to the article, spent most of the interview kissing and touching each other in extravagant displays of affection.

Preston denied that there were any wedding bells in the future – 'Don't say the "m" word,' she told them – but said they were very happy in their state of cohabiting bliss. Clooney for his part also ruled out marriage though he did seem prepared to make some sort of commitment. 'Let's say it's pretty serious,' he said. 'We bought this house together and we have the pig. The most important thing in my life right now is my relationship with Kelly,' said Clooney before adding as a joke, 'and my relationship with Max.'

The article ended with a stomach-churning pun about Clooney and Preston's love being here to sty. But in fact all was not sweetness and light. Although Preston maintained their relationship was based on mutual communication, it became obvious that something was seriously wrong. Within a matter of months of that article appearing Clooney and Preston had split up.

Neither Clooney nor Preston has gone on record at any length about the break-up of their relationship. Her often-quoted suggestion that she was turned off by Clooney's tolerance of Max sharing their bedroom can't be taken seriously as a reason for splitting up. Both appeared to agree that it was simply not working out and the relationship had to end. Clooney may have been resentful of her career, which was about to take off in 'A' list movies while he was stuck in television, but that seems unlikely. That would require a meanness of spirit which does not appear to be borne out in conversation with anyone who knows him.

After the split Kelly Preston got engaged to actor Charlie Sheen in the spring of 1989 and would then go on to marry John Travolta, whom she met later that year on the set of *The Experts*. By the end of the year George Clooney would be married to Talia Balsam. Max, the pig, stayed with Clooney.

'There is a part of George which is sad when it comes to love,' says his long-time friend Tommy Hinckley. 'It's almost as if he feels that with his success he doesn't deserve to have a woman in his life as well. It's as if a person isn't allowed to have both.'

Chapter 11: Then Tragedy Struck

There is an old saying to the effect that you should always be careful what you wish for in case you get it. George Clooney, in whatever moments of quiet contemplation he allowed himself, might have reflected on the wisdom of that saying at this particular point in his life.

Clooney had wanted to be famous. He had wanted to be a performer. He had wanted a Hollywood lifestyle. He wanted the pool and the tennis court and all the trappings of fame and fortune which he had seen at Aunt Rosemary's place when he was a youngster. Now he had them but his life did not seem much enriched by any of it.

The money was great but the work was unsatisfying. The house was luxurious by the standards of some places he had lived in but modest enough by Hollywood standards. On the other hand it was an empty existence without the person he had bought the house with. Life with Max the pot-bellied pig obviously wasn't any kind of substitute for a stable relationship.

It was at this point that George Clooney once again ran into Talia Balsam and they started seeing each other again. This second meeting with Balsam was a fairly typical occurrence for Clooney. Although he has acquired a – he says unjustified – reputation as a lady killer, his is not the technique of the lounge lizard Lothario. Clooney insists that his relationships evolve organically over a period of time. 'People find it hard to believe but I have never formally asked a woman out,' he insists. 'I've always gone out with people I knew. That's easier for me. I used to work as a disc jockey and I'd watch guys go up and hit on a girl and use lines like "Hey, you want to dance and see my moves?" Then I'd see the girls take those guys and pummel them. Women are amazing and I love them,' says Clooney, 'but I realised then that I was never going to give any girl that kind of power.'

With Talia Balsam there was never any danger of it being a relationship of power games and control trips. Clooney knew her of old and he had never really got over their break-up five years previously. She was as close as anyone could come to being the love of his life. At a time when he had just broken up with Kelly Preston it was natural that Clooney would gravitate towards an old friend. For her part Balsam was able to provide more than just moral support. The careers which had got in the way first time round were now well established, leaving the relationship to run its course on a level playing field.

Before too long Clooney proposed. News of their engagement was broken in *People* magazine in October 1989. This was the same magazine which only eight months earlier had run the at-home piece with Clooney and Preston. 'I had gotten out of a relationship that wasn't going very well and married the one girl I truly loved and had loved for years,' says Clooney.

The wedding itself was as weird and unconventional as they come. Clooney, his bride-to-be and a bunch of their friends loaded up a camper van and headed east from Los Angeles to Nevada. 'I went to Vegas with all my friends and got married in a chapel by an Elvis impersonator,' he says. 'I took a Winnebago there. When you come from Kentucky any kind of white-trash thing like that really impresses you.'

The Elvis wedding ceremony was just the beginning of what was to be a wild night. After he had got married Clooney started drinking and then hit the gaming rooms. He spent his wedding night drinking and shooting craps. Later he said that at the time he was reasoning that having taken the big gamble, how much more did he have to lose? On even the most superficial examination any bridegroom should be able to tell that a craps table in Las Vegas is no place to spend your wedding night. Obviously a gambler, Clooney must have realised even then that no one in the room would have given long odds on a marriage surviving such an inauspicious beginning.

It's very hard for any marriage to survive the pressures of two people trying to pursue their separate careers. It's even harder when the careers are as high profile as Clooney's and Balsam's. He was still trying to find that one elusive hit television series which would provide him with the springboard to success. She on the other hand was trying to pursue her career in the theatre. No matter which of them was doing better at any given time, it is not an atmosphere conducive to sitting down and picking colour schemes for the kitchen or wondering what flowers should go in the garden.

In the middle of all this Clooney had signed on to do *Baby Talk* for Ed Weinberger. The ABC series had been inspired by the success of *Look Who's Talking*. Originally the role taken by Kirstie Alley in the movie was taken by Connie Sellecca, who was still a major TV name on the back of her role in the series *Hotel*. But although Sellecca played the female lead in the pilot she had gone before the pilot actually made it to the screen. When the series was picked up her role was taken by Julia Duffy, who also left. In the midst of this procession of leading ladies Clooney remained constant. He played the John Travolta role. In the movie Travolta had been a cab driver, in the TV series Clooney was a construction worker who was working on renovating and refurbishing Sellecca/Duffy's apartment.

'There were a lot of problems on the set,' says Clooney, referring to his difficulties with executive producer Ed Weinberger. 'We had several infamous fights. At some point I just said "You know what? You can't pay me enough to be treated like this." So I stood up for myself.'

Although by this stage George Clooney had been in Los Angeles seven years, he hadn't really changed that much. He was still, not too deep down, living proof that you can take the boy out of the small town but you can't take the small town out of the boy. Laura Laycock, who knows him as well as anyone outside his own family, believes that no matter what happens, George Clooney is and always will be a small town boy.

But she means it in the best possible way. 'I told George the last time he was home,' she explains. 'I said to him "Thank God you grew up in a small town because that goes with you wherever you are."'

Granted Clooney may have stood up to Weinberger because he was tired of his behaviour and growing increasingly frustrated in a bad show which seemed only to be getting worse. But there is also a Gary Cooper quality to his action. It was not the outburst of a prima donna, it was just a man who had been raised to treat people properly and could no longer stand for people being treated badly. Clooney had mentally drawn his line in the sand and Weinberger had unconsciously stepped across it.

It was a gesture which, at the time, convinced Clooney that his career was finished. But it was also a gesture which was not forgotten by those who were there at the time. 'I still run into people from that show and they treat me as if I did something really nice for them. But it wasn't for them,' he admits candidly. 'It was purely selfish. I was a hothead at that point and I just thought "No more!" But I really did think I had ended my career. I thought it was over.'

Of course, as recounted in the opening chapter, Clooney was only out of work for four days before Gary David Goldberg offered him the *Knights of the Kitchen* pilot. There were other offers on top of that, all from people who wanted to thumb their nose, however circumspectly, at Weinberger by offering Clooney work.

Clooney still had a chip on his shoulder, though. What he really wanted to be was a movie star. After his one-liner in *Return of the Killer Tomatoes*, Clooney played a slightly larger role in *Red Surf*. In this 1990 movie Clooney played a former surfing champ who is now running drugs. He and his friends are keen to get out of the business and go straight but another member of the gang turns on them. Clooney's pregnant girlfriend was played by DeDee Pfeiffer – sister of Michelle – and *Kiss* frontman-turned-actor Gene Simmons was also in the film. Although it was a slightly more auspicious production than *Return of the Killer Tomatoes*, *Red Surf* went straight to video. It now doesn't even have *Killer Tomatoes'* comfort of being bad enough for cult status. *Red Surf* appears to have been simply forgettable.

There were other attempts at screen stardom. These were more main-stream. In the summer of the previous year director Ridley Scott had been impressed by Clooney's audition for his feminist road movie *Thelma and Louise*. However, in the end the part of the drifter who charms his way into Geena Davis' life and then makes off with her money went to Brad Pitt. Clooney had missed out on another star-making part. But worse was to come.

A few weeks after the Weinberger incident Clooney met Quentin Tarantino, who was then an unknown writer desperate for his break into the industry with a crime thriller he was directing himself. Tarantino wanted Clooney to audition for one of the gang members but, coming so soon after the experience of *Baby Talk*, Clooney's heart wasn't really in it. 'I did read for *Reservoir Dogs*,' remembers Clooney, 'but I did a horrible audition. Quentin had seen some horrible movie that I had done and he liked me and I was walking into that audition from a good place. But I did a really horrible, horrible audition. I remember walking out and saying to myself "Well, I blew that!"'

Clooney was quite right. He had blown the audition big time and another potential breakthrough had gone the same way as *Thelma and Louise* and *The Breakfast Club*. But Clooney also admits that one of the reasons for performing so poorly in the *Reservoir Dogs* audition was because of his inner turmoil.

He realised by this stage in 1991 that his marriage with Talia Balsam simply wasn't working. The strain of his failing marriage and the added stress of a career which he now had begun to believe was going nowhere was taking its toll. Clooney had put on almost twenty pounds in weight, he had a bleeding ulcer and he was in dreadful shape physically and mentally.

Clooney describes it now, somewhat redundantly, as 'a very tough time'. There was really only one solution and in 1992 after three years of marriage George Clooney and Talia Balsam divorced. It was a relationship which should have been left to die when it ended in 1984. George Clooney had learned the hard way that you can never go back. 'I probably – definitely – was not someone who should have been married at that point,' admits Clooney with hindsight. 'I just don't feel like I gave Talia a fair shot. I was responsible for the failure of that marriage.'

Clooney and Balsam had met in 1984. They had been friends for almost ten years by the time they were divorced in 1992. Clooney was willing to accept the bulk of the responsibility for the marriage not working and he was hoping for a reasonably amicable and civilised divorce. That's not how things worked out in practice. Inevitably there were lawyers involved and rancour crept in all round. 'I would say to Talia "You tell me how much. What you think is fair – I'll write the cheque." I won't negotiate,' recalls Clooney. 'Instead, I paid $80,000 in lawyers' fees and that makes me angry.'

There is no doubt that George Clooney loved Talia Balsam. Whether he loved her for as long or as deeply as he thought he did is another matter. Their first break-up hurt him badly. Their divorce left him forswearing marriage forever. 'I suppose I've failed over the years at relationships,' he said recently. 'I never thought of them as total failures, though. If you stay together in this business for any length of time, you've kind of won. I'll never be married again and I'll never have kids,' he says. 'From my point of view the biggest part of why my marriage didn't work was my fault. I married a terrific girl, a great lady, but it didn't work out. I don't take full responsibility for that but when things were starting to go wrong I wasn't willing to try to fix them,' he continues. 'I just wanted to chuck the whole thing and that is not the way you should be in a marriage.'

Clooney was obviously hurt by the break-up of his marriage. But there were others who were hurt too. Talia Balsam of course. But George Clooney's parents felt it keenly too. They had long since got over their disapproval with their son's career choice by this stage. In fact they had moved to Los Angeles themselves, where Nick Clooney was working as a local news anchor. He had also hosted a short-lived game show for the ABC network. But they were genuinely fond of Talia Balsam and were distressed by the divorce.

'Talia is a lovely girl,' says Nick Clooney. 'But they probably shouldn't have got married while George's career was on the verge of such a white-hot period. I know George blames himself for the divorce, which is characteristically gallant of him. But he's too tough on himself. In truth, neither of them was to blame. There was just too much going on in their lives to give marriage the effort it needs. They both wound up getting hurt which is really too bad. Now George says he's never going to get married again, doesn't want kids, and doesn't even want a serious relationship with a woman.'

However, Nick Clooney is maintaining a degree of scepticism about his son's bold declaration. 'I know George,' he continues, 'and I know some great woman is going to come along and knock him right off his feet. He will be a great husband and father. Though I hope he waits until he is at a point in his career where he can devote himself to a relationship. This is not that time, and George knows it.'

Chapter 12:
A Death in the
Family

The break-up of his marriage affected George Clooney deeply. But the break-up itself may only have been a symptom of something much deeper and much more troubling. His divorce may well have been prompted by something else which cut Clooney to the bone and changed his life in the process.

Uncle George had died.

For Clooney it was a loss felt as keenly as if it had been his own father. In many ways Uncle George had been a surrogate father for the boy who was named after him and was more like him than perhaps he cared to admit. Uncle George had been one of the keystones of George Clooney's youth. It was Uncle George who had taught him to stand up for himself against the Ed Weinbergers of this world. It was Uncle George who had taught him to believe in himself and not to take any bullshit from anyone.

George Clooney was there when Uncle George died. The old man had never married and had no children of his own. He looked on George – his grand-nephew – as a son, and, like a good son should, Clooney had gone to visit Uncle George when he was back home to see friends and neighbours in Augusta. Years of drinking, hard-living, and self-neglect had taken their toll. He had prematurely aged and the once dashing war hero who flew all those bombing missions was now drawn and haggard. His trademark was no longer his good looks and his roguish repartee; now it was a hacking cough. George took one look at the old man and ordered him to hospital.

The doctors could tell almost by looking at him. But he was admitted and within 24 hours the tests came back to confirm what everyone already knew and privately dreaded. Uncle George had lung cancer. It was wide-spread, deep-seated and inoperable. His reaction was typical, according to young George. He asked for a cigarette. 'They told him "You've got it everywhere,"' said Clooney when he was able to talk about it some years later. 'And I think he just said "I quit."'

Uncle George stopped fighting. He simply gave up the ghost and not long afterwards he died in George Clooney's arms. He was 64 years old.

George Clooney is not an emotional man. He is slow to anger, he is reluctant to express his feelings and he is the last man in the world to wear his heart on his sleeve. The bluff exterior which he presents to the outside world masks a much more thoughtful interior where emotions are internalised and penned in. This, presumably, is one of the reasons why he had been suffering from a bleeding ulcer. People who are good at dealing with their emotions and confronting their feelings tend not to have ulcers. These tend to be the preserve of those who bottle things up to be dealt with at some future, unspecified date.

Uncle George's death affected George Clooney deeply. It was one of the pivotal events in his life. The two were close and Clooney resolved to learn a lesson from Uncle George in death as he had in life. 'I said "I'm not gonna wake up at 64 and say 'What a waste,'"' he recalled. 'I just decided life was too short. I decided that if I walked outside and got hit by a bus then at least everybody can say "He crammed a shitload into 34 years."'

It was Uncle George's death that encouraged Clooney to seize the day. He was going to live for the moment. If a job wasn't going right – like *Baby Talk* – then he would just walk away from it. If his relationships weren't working – like the ones with Kelly Preston and Talia Balsam – then he would walk away from them too. He wasn't going to spend the time to fix something that was broken, he was just going to get a new one. It didn't really matter whether that was a job, a woman or a car.

It's an extraordinarily selfish point of view from someone who – by the accounts of people who know him well – is an extraordinarily generous man. Talk to anyone about Clooney and the last adjective they will use is selfish. 'Woody Allen once said that success gives people the permission to become exactly who they were always meant to be,' says *Batman and Robin* director and Clooney fan Joel Schumacher. 'Some people when they get successful, punish everyone. Others, like George, are grateful. George is extraordinarily generous,' says Schumacher while refusing to elaborate on Clooney's private benevolences. 'It used to be called character. He has seen it all. Because he is so attractive, he has been invited to all the parties. All the women stars know who he is. He has seen a lot of people self-destruct'.

Clooney need look no further than his own Aunt Rosemary for evidence of how fame can destroy someone without warning. His outburst of self-centred hedonism following the death of Uncle George and the end of his marriage appears to have been a fairly short-lived expression of rage. It may possibly have been short-lived because he had seen first hand what that kind of behaviour can ultimately cause. And it is also more likely because he had good friends there to look after him.

When he first came to Los Angeles Clooney became fast friends with other struggling actors like Tom Matthews and Tommy Hinkley. Throughout his ups and downs they remained his friends and they show a fierce mutual loyalty. They were there when his marriage ended and they were more than willing to join in the round of post-divorce hi-jinks to celebrate his newly regained bachelor status. But they were also there to let him know that enough was enough and it was time to get back in the saddle, career-wise.

Although he hadn't blown his career as he had feared in the public spat with Ed Weinberger, George Clooney was entitled to fear that his career had at the very least stalled. There were the pilots of course and there were guest star spots in other shows too. In his time Clooney has guested on shows like *Golden Girls*, *Murder She Wrote*, *Hunter*, *Nightmare Café* and many others. He was always a popular choice to come in and do a bit on anyone's show.

There was even another movie. In 1992 Clooney starred in *Unbecoming Age*, a romantic comedy-fantasy. Directed by Deborah and Alfredo Ringel, it starred Diane Salinger as a women who becomes bored and depressed when she turns 40. With the aid of some "magic bubbles" which she blows, she is able to recapture her youth and vigour. George Clooney was part of an ensemble cast which also included Wallace Shawn, Colleen Camp and Nicholas Guest. However, *Unbecoming Age* appears to have been as light and insubstantial as one of Salinger's magic bubbles and did not get a cinematic release. In that respect it fared no better than any of Clooney's previous films.

But guest spots and movies no one saw do not constitute a career. There was still no sign of that elusive, star-making, career-defining role. By this stage George Clooney had rapidly become what his cousin Miguel Ferrer described as the wealthiest unknown actor in television. Clooney himself had perhaps begun to realise that he was never going to get the chance to do major features. He could no longer pretend to himself that he was a movie actor who just happened to be stuck in television. Maybe *Red Surf* and *Unbecoming Age* were as good as his movie career was ever going to get. It was very hard to come to terms with that. Looking back Clooney admits that it was almost impossible. 'I had a beautiful house then and the greatest friends in the whole world,' he says as he reflects on one of the most difficult periods in his life. 'I had a great time. I did. But you get lost a little bit. Towards the end of my twenties was a really bad time for me.'

The one thing you don't get to do in small towns is feel sorry for yourself. For one thing, no one will let you. For another you learn to take charge of your own life. So, not for the first time, Clooney had to dust himself off and start all over again. By this stage he had done a dozen failed pilots and starred in five different television series. If nothing else he was starting to hone his instincts for what was good and what was not. 'I've always had a fairly good eye for what I was doing,' says Clooney without any trace of false modesty. 'I could tell myself "Hey, this is a piece of fluff but I'm going to make some nice money," or "Oh man, this is really something special."'

Clooney now had the choice to put those instincts to the test. If, as he now feared, he was going to have to stay in television then he would have to do good television. In 1992 he was offered the choice of two series. He could star in *Café Americain* which was a vehicle for Valerie Bertinelli, or he could take a role in *Sisters*, an ensemble comedy-drama starring Swoosie Kurtz and Sela Ward. Clooney was not going to be top banana in either show; both Bertinelli and Kurtz were established TV names and they were the notional stars of the show.

Clooney decided to go with *Sisters*. It was a perceptive choice. *Café Americain* lasted eight weeks before it was cancelled. *Sisters* went on to be a solid hit.

In American television, ratings and demographics are everything – no one knew that better than George Clooney, who had learned as a child just what a difference the numbers can mean. When he famously described Clooney's greatest asset as his ass, NBC vice-president Warren Littlefield was not being as demeaning as he might have appeared. He was merely articulating, albeit a little crudely, the demonstrable fact that Clooney's key demographic was largely female. How could it be anything else given his looks and that charm? As Littlefield said, they had noticed it with *The Facts of Life*. And it continued through *Roseanne* and even the dreadful *Baby Talk*. Women loved to watch George Clooney.

Sisters was no exception. The stories of female sibling rivalry meant that the show was skewed towards women and the show's overwhelmingly female audience began to notice the same thing as Warren Littlefield. They simply could not get enough of Clooney, who was playing the recurring role of Sela Ward's romantic interest. On screen Ward and Clooney made a very fetching couple and audiences wanted to see more of them – or more specifically more of Clooney. The script writers were under instructions to include more of Clooney whenever possible and his part grew and grew to the point where he was worked into the show wherever possible.

All of this was grist to Clooney's mill. *Sisters* was a good show. It had a quality cast, it was pulling down reasonable numbers and it was getting good reviews too. What's more, there was none of the friction or the unpleasantness which had characterised Clooney's experiences on *Baby Talk*.

Sela Ward, who had to play most often opposite Clooney, was, and still is, a big admirer of his talent and his attitude. 'When we were on the set all bummed out to be there at six in the morning,' she recalls, 'George would come into the trailer and have us in stitches. We miss him terribly.'

There was a downside to appearing in *Sisters*, as far as Clooney was concerned. He was getting a little worried about how his character was developing. As essentially the only man in an all-female cast he was legitimately worried about his character being stereotyped. Also, with the writers under instructions to include him at almost every turn, he was rapidly running out of things that his character could do.

By the end of 1993, after a year on the show, Clooney made it clear that he did not see *Sisters* in his long-term plans. 'It's a chick show,' he said, not unkindly. 'As a guy you become all of those horrible parts, women's parts, that women have complained about for years and have every right to complain about.'

So, faced with the choice of quitting or becoming what he perceived to be not much more than a 'himbo', George Clooney left the show.

For the second time in his career George Clooney had turned his back on what he felt was the big break. The first time round, on *Roseanne*, it had triggered a three-year cycle of professional and personal misery. Now, having got back to the top, he was ready to leave again. This time it would be for a period of unprecedented and unparalleled success.

'George was handicapped by his looks,' says *ER* executive producer John Wells. 'There was always a sense that he was going to be a star, that's why he did so many pilots. He jumped off the screen as a great guy. But with anyone that cute and personable it was hard to tell whether he had any acting chops.'

Neither George Clooney nor John Wells knew that Wells' question was about to be answered in a very big way.

Chapter 13: Five Patients

No actor takes a decision to quit a show lightly, especially if the show is a successful one. Actors live between chance and oblivion and only the very lucky ones have never experienced the pain of rejection and the anguish of uncertainty about where the next job – and many times the next meal – is coming from. All of these factors come into play when the decision is made to turn down what might well be a long-standing meal ticket.

George Clooney had already left one top-rated show, now he was leaving another. The reasons for his departure from *Sisters*, however, were vastly different from his reasons for leaving *Roseanne*. All actors have a sixth sense which tells them whether they are succeeding in a part or not. No matter what the critics say actors know how good a job they are really doing in. With *Roseanne*, Clooney knew that he really wasn't right for the role. Audiences loved Booker and that was part of the problem, they were supposed to dislike him, he was the bad guy after all. The role just wasn't working, Clooney couldn't overcome his own natural appeal, and despite the writers' best efforts he believed he had made the right decision in leaving.

With *Sisters*, however, he couldn't have been any more right for the part. He had been a huge popular and critical success as Sela Ward's romantic interest and was occasionally threatening to eclipse the nominal stars of the show in popularity. But he knew that he had to go because, even though he was right for the part, he had done everything he could. All that was left was for him to keep doing the same things he had been doing over and over again.

But leaving *Sisters* was the right thing to do. You could argue that, at the stage he was at in his career at that time, he might have toughed it out for another season in *Roseanne* for the sake of visibility and experience. However, there is no faulting Clooney's decision to quit *Sisters*. And the industry agreed with him. Eyebrows might have been raised when he left *Roseanne* but the movers and shakers in the television industry knew that his decision to leave the female ensemble show had been inevitable.

'*Sisters* helped me out a great deal,' says Clooney looking back on his time in the show. 'For one thing it got me back "in" at NBC which I hadn't been for a while.'

In fact, although Clooney had worked for all three major networks, he had not done a show for NBC since *The Facts of Life*. But NBC knew that Clooney was now almost the finished article, so too did Warner Brothers who had made *Sisters* and still had him under contract. Clooney had proved that he could play drama when he had to – it wasn't all laughs on *Sisters* – and he had once again proved that he could deliver an audience.

But *Sisters* did more for Clooney than simply get him back into favour with a television network. It did something significant to his attitude. It was *Sisters* which helped him lose the chip on his shoulder about really being a movie actor deep down but being trapped in television in the meantime. This was a quality show and it was attracting high numbers and good reviews, for him especially. Clooney began to realise that the way to a movie career was not in low-budget quickies which would never be released. Much better to build on what he had. Clooney had an enormous amount of clout in the television industry by this stage. He was still a hot actor, he strolled around the Warner Brothers sound stages in Burbank like the college bowl winning quarterback. He was a popular guy. He would use that popularity and his influence with people like Warren Littlefield to make sure he did better-quality television and then use that as a launch pad to a movie career. Bruce Willis had done it from *Moonlighting*, Clint Eastwood had done it from *Rawhide* before that. All he needed was the right television show.

When George Clooney was still in primary school Michael Crichton was finishing his studies at Harvard Medical School. Crichton had been born John Michael Crichton in Chicago on October 23, 1942. He was always determined to be a doctor but, not being independently wealthy, had to find a way to finance himself through medical school. Crichton financed his education by writing. Under a series of pseudonyms such as Jeffrey Hudson and John Lange he wrote a number of thrillers based on his own medical experience. The one which finally made it big for him was *The*

Andromeda Strain, which he wrote and published in 1969 under his own name, just before he graduated from medical school. The book was a huge success and was sold to Hollywood to be turned into a Robert Wise movie two years later.

Crichton was still a student doctor when *The Andromeda Strain* was published and, like all medical students, had spent more hours than he cared to think about in the trenches of the emergency room. The emergency room is the first point of contact with the hospital for most patients. All human life is there and time spent on duty here is the most testing time of a doctor's career.

Since he was at Harvard, Crichton did his training at the busy Massachusetts General Hospital. Crichton was fascinated by the pace, the drama, the humour, the sheer vibrancy of the emergency room. His time spent here became the basis for his non-fiction book *Five Patients*, which was first published in 1970.

Although he graduated in 1969 Crichton was destined not to spend very long practising medicine. His intelligent but pacy techno-thrillers became more and more sophisticated and more and more popular. Having sold one to Hollywood it was inevitable that he would sell more and soon he found himself as a full-time novelist. It was a short step from there to becoming more actively involved in the whole process.

In 1972 Michael Crichton stepped behind the camera for the first time to make his directing debut with *Pursuit*. This was a television movie which had been adapted from Crichton's own novel *Binary*, written under the pen-name John Lange. The film starred Ben Gazzarra, E.G. Marshall and Martin Sheen, with Gazzarra the government agent trying to prevent a terrorist from destroying a city with a deadly nerve gas. *Pursuit* was well received and in the nature of such things Crichton's film career was up and running.

Whether he was writing or directing, and occasionally he was doing both, Crichton quickly built up an impressive list of critical and commercial successes which included *Westworld*, *The Terminal Man*, *Coma*, and *The First Great Train Robbery*. He very soon established himself as a leading Hollywood 'hyphenate'. In his case he was a writer-director.

But medicine remained Crichton's first love and his abiding interest. He kept himself at the cutting edge of research and used his books and films to alert people to what he saw as the dangers inherent in medicine; the over-reliance on computers in *The Terminal Man*, for example, or the use of patients as donor organ banks in *Coma*. He still felt that the hurly burly and drama of his days in the emergency room which he had put down in *Five*

Patients had the basis of a good movie. By this stage he had his own reputation to back him up and he had also found someone who was rapidly becoming a powerful ally.

One of the first people Michael Crichton met when he came to Hollywood was a young intern at Universal Studios. The intern had got a job at the studios by simply walking through the gates every day with enough authority to convince the security guards that he really belonged there. After weeks hanging around various sets and watching people work he was eventually rumbled. However, the studio was so impressed with his nerve and his desire to break into the business that he was taken on at the lowest level on the career ladder. And that's how Steven Spielberg came to be showing Michael Crichton around Universal after *The Andromeda Strain* had been bought by the studio to turn into a movie.

The two men were similarly ambitious and were each impressed by the other's enthusiasms. Spielberg has a fascination for technology and science and Crichton's erudite and articulate theories about the future of modern medicine found an eager ear in the younger man. The two became fast friends and have remained so till this day.

In 1974 Crichton had finally turned *Five Patients* into a screenplay. It was known as *EW* – for Emergency Ward – and it charted 24 hours in the lives of the patients and staff in the casualty department of a major metropolitan hospital. Despite his success and the influence of people like Steven Spielberg, who was now the most influential director in Hollywood, *EW* remained resolutely unproduced.

'I wanted to write something that was based in reality,' Crichton would say later. 'Something that would have a fast pace and treat medicine in a realistic way. The screenplay was very unusual. It was very focused on the doctors, not the patients – the patients came and went. People yelled paragraphs of drug dosages at each other. It was very technical, almost a quasi-documentary. But what interested me was breaking standard dramatic structure. I understood that's what the screenplay did, but I always felt that it was compulsively watchable.'

However, not many people shared Crichton's view. There were occasions when the film came close to being made but Crichton was always reluctant to compromise. He was unwilling to make the changes that were almost always requested. He refused to smooth off the rough edges and make it a more homogenised medical thriller. 'In a certain way,' he said later, 'I always felt it was in a special category, a strange thing that was on its own with nothing else like it. Of course when there isn't anything else like it, that's a very difficult animal in the world of entertainment. Something that breaks the rules is looked on with suspicion.'

Throughout the Eighties Crichton continued his career, primarily as a novelist but with occasional films like *Looker*, *Runaway* and *Physical Evidence*. Spielberg for his part was maturing as a director as well as becoming one of the most successful producers in Hollywood. Towards the end of the Eighties he felt like doing something a little more serious and heavyweight after his *Indiana Jones* trilogy. One of the ideas which had grabbed his attention was Michael Crichton's script about life in an emergency room. So Spielberg bought the script – which was now called *ER* – with the intention of making it his next film.

Fifteen years after it had been written back in 1974 it looked as if the film version of *Five Patients* would finally see the light of day. But there were still more obstacles in its path as both Spielberg and Crichton became sidetracked on the biggest project of their career.

During script revision meetings for the *Five Patients* movie in 1989, Crichton was continuing to work on his new novel. When the subject of what he was working on came up in conversation Crichton mentioned that he was researching a book about the possibility of cloning dinosaurs from prehistoric DNA. Spielberg was fascinated and, after pumping Crichton for as much information as he could, he said he wanted to make it into a movie. Crichton realised through years of friendship that Spielberg was the only man with the vision and daring to bring his book to the screen and agreed there and then that there was no one he would rather see direct it.

The agreement was sealed with a handshake and what had started as a script meeting for *ER* ended up as the first pre-production meeting on *Jurassic Park*.

ER was put on the back burner as *Jurassic Park* went onto the fast track. Crichton continued with his novel and then the screenplay from his own book. Spielberg made his Peter Pan story *Hook* and then threw himself into bringing the Jurassic era back to life. Spielberg and Crichton were about to enter one of the most fertile periods of their creative lives. After *Jurassic Park*, Spielberg went straight into *Schindler's List* – he was working on both pictures at the same time at one stage – which left him so drained he was unable to contemplate directing anything else for more than a year. Crichton for his part had followed up the phenomenal sales of *Jurassic Park*, his most successful book to date, with two more controversial best-sellers. *Rising Sun* was about the influence of Japanese corporate life on America and *Disclosure* was another headline-grabber about sexual harassment in the workplace. Crichton's spin came in making it the male executive rather than the female who was being harassed. Both books went on to be hugely successful films with Crichton keenly involved as screenwriter on *Rising Sun* and producer on *Disclosure*.

It began to seem as though Crichton's much-loved pet project was going to become a victim of his own success. The international best-selling author and top-ranked producer simply didn't have the time to make a movie out of the book he had written on his days as a struggling medical student.

There was one more chance. Steven Spielberg was a man of considerable influence in Hollywood and he used that influence and patronage to produce other people's films as well as directing his own. He has been responsible for the careers of directors like Robert Zemeckis and Ron Howard as well as phenomenally successful films like *Who Framed Roger Rabbit?* and the *Back to the Future* series. By the middle of the Eighties he had diversified his production skills into television.

Spielberg was responsible for *Amazing Stories*, a short-form fantasy anthology series which was popular in syndication, *Tiny Toons* which was a very successful animated series and *SeaQuest DSV*, a big budget underwater science-fiction series. All of these shows were produced under the umbrella of Spielberg's Amblin Television.

It was in October of 1993 that Amblin's president of television Tony Thomopoulos came up with an idea which was brilliant in its simplicity. He came across Michael Crichton's script for *ER* and suggested that they forget about doing it as a movie and turn it into a weekly television series instead.

Chapter 14:
e.r.

*T*rying to do *ER* as a weekly television series certainly meant that Michael Crichton's vision stood a slightly better chance of coming to the screen now that it was no longer languishing in development hell in a studio. But it still had a great many hurdles in its path before audiences could share Crichton's view of hospital life.

For one thing there was the climate of the time as far as hit television shows were concerned. The notion to do *ER* as a TV show was first mooted in October 1993, a couple of months into the 1993-4 television season. One major difficulty was that, at that time, hour-long dramas were simply not in vogue. Television runs in fads. When George Clooney was growing up, for example, the hour-long Western – *Bonanza, Wagon Train, Cheyenne* and *Gunsmoke* – reigned supreme. In the Seventies it was fast-moving cop shows like *Starsky and Hutch, Charlie's Angels* and *Kojak*. The Eighties had been dominated by glitzy melodrama like *Dallas* and *Dynasty*; these were essentially prime-time soaps but they were still ratings behemoths. But by the Nineties this had all given way to short-form comedy.

The half-hour comedy show, ideally as a vehicle for a single star, was the ratings king. If you look at the top ten shows for the 1992-3 American TV season – the season just ended when Thomopoulos made his *ER* suggestion – six of the top ten shows were half- hour comedies. The exceptions were the news show *60 Minutes*, Angela Lansbury's crime series *Murder She Wrote*, the live NFL game on Monday nights and the *CBS Sunday Night Movie*. Otherwise the ratings were dominated by *Roseanne, Home Improvement, Murphy Brown, Coach, Cheers* and *Full House*. Indeed, in the whole top twenty there wasn't a single show that could be considered as a heavyweight drama – the closest any of them came were *Murder She Wrote* and *Northern Exposure*.

The following season – the one in which Amblin thought about doing *ER* – didn't show any improvement as far as drama was concerned. The half-hour comedies were actually increasing their stranglehold. Tim Allen's *Home Improvement* had replaced *60 Minutes* as the nation's top show and the only other non-comedy shows in the top ten were again *Murder She Wrote* and *Monday Night Football* and these had slipped to the bottom two places. In the 1993-4 television season there were now seven comedies among America's ten favourite shows. Apart from *Home Improvement*, the other top-rating series were *Seinfeld, Roseanne, Grace Under Fire, These Friends of Mine* – which would become *Ellen* – *Frasier* and *Coach*. The shows may have changed but the trend remained the same and that was a daunting prospect for *ER*'s chances.

There was, however, a small chink of light in those ratings. Creeping in at number 18 and 19 respectively in the 1993-4 season were *NYPD Blue* and *Homicide: Life on the Streets*. The first show was a controversial new offering from ace producer Steven Bochco which took a gritty and uncompromising look at the life of New York cops. The show's strong language and occasional discreet nudity – tame by European standards but shocking by the standards of American television – had made it something of a cause célèbre. *Homicide: Life on the Streets* was an equally hard-nosed show produced by movie director Barry Levinson. This time the focus was on Baltimore detectives. The rather cumbersome title came as a result of two similar shows being developed at the same time. Lorimar had been developing a cop show called *Homicide* which, ironically, was to have starred George Clooney, but it never materialised.

A weekly drama series of any description was going to be a difficult nut for Amblin to crack. It was going to be even more difficult given the fact that Steven Spielberg's success rate on television was nowhere near as good as his track record in the cinema. While *Tiny Toons* was a great success with children and *Amazing Stories* was popular in syndication, he had yet to have a major ratings success in mainstream television. Despite the heavyweight presence of actors of the calibre of Roy Scheider, his futuristic underwater fantasy *SeaQuest DSV* was proving a failure. Industry insiders had cruelly dubbed the show 'Voyage to the Bottom of the Ratings' because of its poor performance.

There were also those at Amblin who were concerned about whether or not *ER* would make it as a weekly show. Chief among them was Michael

Crichton. Although he obviously wanted his pet project made he was also concerned about preserving its integrity. He was interested in the notion of a weekly television version of *Five Patients* but worried that his original concept might have to be so diluted to accommodate the networks that it would be almost meaningless. And there is no doubt that, as written, Crichton's *ER* script was going to be a difficult one to bring off. It was two hours long, it had 87 scenes and more than a hundred speaking parts. Any one of these three factors would have made a television company baulk at the prospect, the combination of all three was asking a great deal of any network.

Nonetheless Amblin pressed ahead. After a series of meetings it was agreed that the production chores would be handled by Amblin in association with Crichton's own production company, Constant Productions, and Warner Brothers Television. Then after a further series of meetings, NBC television gave the go-ahead for a two-hour pilot.

At a very early stage in the proceedings, Tony Thomopoulos had brought in John Wells to join Michael Crichton in the discussions about his baby. Wells was a successful television writer and producer whose most recent show, *China Beach* – a drama about nurses in Vietnam – had been a huge critical hit without being an enormous ratings success. Wells' background in television drama and his recent expertise with a medical show seemed like the ideal combination. From a very early stage in its proposed television development, Wells was able to troubleshoot Crichton's script and identify the areas which were going to prove problematic.

'One of the chief complaints about the script was that you didn't know who you were supposed to care about,' Wells explains in the book *Behind the Scenes at ER*. 'There wasn't a beginning, a middle, or an end. There was just a series of small scenes. It had multiple story lines, and many stories which just had one beat and didn't go anywhere else. There was very little standard dramatic through line.'

That should really not have come as any surprise. Crichton wanted *ER* to resemble as much as possible life in a real casualty ward. Real life is notoriously long on incident and short on plot, so Crichton's reflection of it would appear to be the same.

But for all his constructive criticism, Wells could also see the virtues of doing *ER* like this. In many ways it resembled his own *China Beach*, where the whole was much greater than the sum of the individual parts. '*ER* was like a pointillist painting,' says Wells. 'Looking closely at the bits and pieces of scenes they seemed not to make sense. But when you stepped back they added up to an emotional tapestry which was very moving.'

With the commitment from NBC to a two-hour pilot, work on *ER* could begin in earnest. The hospital drama has been a staple of American television for years. When George Clooney was born, Richard Chamberlain's *Dr Kildare* and Vince Edwards' *Ben Casey* were the nation's favourite medics. Casey and Kildare vied for the ascendancy and although *Dr Kildare* was the more popular, both made the top twenty and each had their own large and enthusiastic band of followers. The Seventies saw former Hollywood star Robert Young as *Marcus Welby M.D.*, in the Eighties Jack Klugman played a crusading medical examiner in *Quincy*, and rising stars like Denzel Washington, David Morse and Alfred Woodard cut their acting teeth in *St Elsewhere*. Throughout all of this the daytime soap *General Hospital* continued to be one of America's most enduring and longest-running television programmes.

There was no denying that a good medical show could work, the problem was in making sure that the format could be updated sufficiently to suit modern audiences and satisfy Crichton's concerns about the integrity of his project. Most of *ER*'s predecessors had concentrated on the brilliance of the doctors; whether it was *Dr Kildare*, *Ben Casey* or *Marcus Welby* it was all about their skill in saving the seemingly helpless patient. *ER* wasn't about that. *ER* was about doctors and nurses and the whole milieu of the emergency room; the patients were largely incidental, serving as little more than vehicles for the development of the characters of the *ER* staff. It's hard to imagine Richard Chamberlain or Vince Edwards fitting into this kind of show, but television drama had changed a lot since their day.

The watershed in American television drama came in 1979 when Steven Bochco put *Hill Street Blues* into production. This iconoclastic cop show set new standards for television drama. The focus of the stories was the police and not the criminals. The heroes themselves were a mixed bag; there was the recovering alcoholic Captain Furrillo, the battle-scarred but sensitive Sergeant Eszterhas, the red-neck patrolman Renko and the border-line psychotic Mick Belcker. This was a much richer and exotic cast of characters than television had been used to. The format of the show was vastly different. Unlike *Starsky and Hutch* or *Kojak* where one case would be dealt with from soup to nuts in every episode, *Hill Street Blues* offered a collection of story lines. There were at least three plots going in every episode and, as a rule of thumb, only one was ever resolved per show. It was a challenging and intelligent format and audiences loved it. *Hill Street Blues* was not a massive ratings winner to begin with but it was attracting the sort of discerning audience which advertisers loved so it survived to set a new benchmark in television.

The *Hill Street* format of varied plots, natural sound and lots of background action was developed to great effect by *St Elsewhere*. Again the large ensemble cast of doctors and administrators allowed the writers to weave their storylines in and out of the lives of the characters. And, like Hill Street police station, the hospital in *St Elsewhere* meant there was always a large throughput of characters and incident on a weekly basis.

Hill Street Blues and *St Elsewhere* would lay the groundwork but *ER* would take their efforts and turn them into an art form. Under the guiding hand of John Wells, the show would break new ground and set new standards. But that was still a long way away. There was still the small matter of getting the pilot off the ground.

The pilot is the most important show in any series. That may sound self-evident because if the pilot doesn't succeed then the show won't be picked up. But the function of the pilot is actually more than that. The pilot sets the tone for the series. It should introduce all of the major characters and define who they are and where they are coming from. It becomes the style book, the reference work from which all other episodes derive. It is very rare – *Star Trek* is one of the few exceptions – for a pilot to be picked up as a series and then drastically made over.

The key to a good pilot is the director. At a stage where everything else is by definition untried, the experience of a good director is invaluable. He or she is the person whose judgement will finally decide what goes out to the public. For *ER*, Wells and Crichton wanted the best and they found him in the shape of Rod Holcomb. In a hit and miss industry like television, Holcomb's strike rate is staggering. Prior to *ER* he had directed thirteen pilots and of those thirteen, eleven had been picked up as series. His successes included the pilots for shows like *The Greatest American Hero*, *The A-Team*, *The Equaliser* and – with John Wells – *China Beach*. Wells and Holcomb worked well together and Holcomb shared Wells' enthusiasm for Crichton's project.

'I remember calling John Wells after I'd read the script and saying "I'm exhausted",' recalls Holcomb. 'It was 157 pages long, which is about forty pages longer than a normal pilot script, and it took a tremendous amount of attention to read. But I found it quite interesting. I thought there were some wonderful characters in it. There was a lot of medical verbiage along with the story-telling but as I read it more closely – and had discussions with John and Michael – it became clear that the verbiage was only like a gurney wheel turning. It actually served to motivate the patients and the doctors surrounding them. In years past the story-telling tended to be very pedantic. The story needed to have such exacting explanations made in order to make it credible that often the audience lost the ability to see the main characters. With *ER* it was apparent that the characters were revealed through the fragmented narrative.'

Holcomb was hooked, as indeed almost everyone else had been who came across the project at this stage. With a script, two producers and a director on board, all they needed now was a cast.

They all decided very quickly that George Clooney would be their ideal choice for one of the two leading roles. They wondered whether they could interest him in the part. What they didn't know was that not only was he interested, he was already looking for them to demand the part.

Chapter 15:
Calling Dr Ross

His success in *Sisters* meant that, in television terms at least, the world was pretty much George Clooney's oyster when he left the show. He was still under contract to Warner Television and they were convinced he was perhaps only one show away from becoming the major star they had always believed he would be.

What they were looking for now was a show which would be a vehicle for Clooney. As the actor himself recalls, he was being offered around half a dozen pilots to choose from. The most likely, as far as Warners were concerned, was a cop show called *Golden Gate* in which Clooney would be the headliner and the whole show would be built around him. There was also of course the pilot for *ER*, but that was a part – albeit a large part – in a sizeable ensemble cast.

Clooney's judgement – with the exception of *Baby Talk* – has by and large been very good when it comes to choosing projects. He was once again faced with the sort of choice he had faced when he had to pick between *Café Americain* and *Sisters*. Once again he jumped the right way, but this time he had the inside track when it came to making his decision. An old friend who was a casting director at NBC had slipped him the script for the *ER* pilot while he was still starring in *Sisters* and Clooney knew that this was the one for him. 'I knew,' he says firmly. 'I fought to get *ER*. I didn't think that *ER* was necessarily going to get picked up, because you never know. Some of the best pilots I've done didn't get picked up. I was doing *Sisters* which was a good enough show and fun to be on, but I was just a guest on that show. I was just there. I had a deal at Warner Brothers and they offered me another pilot at NBC that they wanted me to do, but I wanted to do *ER*. I wanted to do it because it was Spielberg, because it was Michael Crichton. It was a two hour movie of the week and at least if it didn't go then I had worked with Spielberg and Crichton.'

'That really amounts to something,' he continues. 'That's a coup for an actor coming from the place I was coming from, which was *Return of the Killer Tomatoes*. So I was hoping – I really fought for it. As I say, I had a deal at Warner Brothers and they said "We'll you'll have to read for it," and I said "I'm happy to read." I went in and I fought for it and at the very least that's what I got out of it – a great movie of the week with these guys. Up to this point, you have to remember, my career had not really been known for doing great television. So I needed some camouflage and a two-hour movie of the week that a lot of people would see, written by Michael Crichton and produced by Steven Spielberg, would make a lot of difference.'

The cast of *ER* is as rich and exotic as *Hill Street Blues* had been some fifteen years earlier. The first season featured no fewer than 31 regular recurring characters with dozens more appearing in two or three episode arcs. The core of the show, however, are the six central characters whose lives we follow most closely.

There is Dr Mark Greene who, as the attending physician, is essentially in charge of the emergency room. Greene is married with a child but the pressures of his job and his wife's legal career may prove insurmountable. His moral opposite is Dr Doug Ross who is the resident paediatrician in the *ER*. Ross is a heavy drinker and a womaniser whose remarkable empathy with children disguises a complete inability to relate to anyone in his personal life.

As the rising, hot-shot surgeon, Dr Peter Benton is a contradiction. He is arrogant and completely lacking in humility. He is a brilliant surgeon with the beginnings of a very unhealthy God complex, but at the same time he tries to care for his ailing mother and help keep his family together. Doing his best to study at his feet is Dr John Carter, the medical student who acts as the audience's conduit into the arcana of the emergency room. Carter is bright and promising but may be crushed under the weight of his responsibilities.

Head nurse Carol Hathaway keeps the emergency room going. She is an exemplary member of the caring profession but she is given to deep periods of introspection and depression. She has a relationship with Doug Ross but is frustrated by his lack of commitment. Rounding out the cast is Dr Susan Lewis, a pragmatic and level-headed young woman who is trying to do her job to the best of her ability while at the same time trying to cope with family pressures, particularly a substance-abusing sister.

The casting of these six roles was absolutely crucial. These half dozen characters would have to work as the central dramatic unit. Each would get their chance to shine in individual episodes or plot lines but they would also have to work as a cohesive team to drive the show along. There would be no room for egos or for prima donnas; everyone would have to be able to work with everyone else.

The first role to be assigned was that of Doug Ross. Clooney had already been slipped a copy of the script and once word had begun to leak out that the pilot had been given the go-ahead he was on the phone to John Wells within 48 hours.

'As soon as the show got a pick-up George called me and said "Doug Ross is my part,"' remembers Wells. 'I hadn't even hired a director at that point but as soon as I hired Rod – which happened to be a Thursday – George called me again and on Friday, he read for the show. He was terrific. Rod gave him a couple of adjustments which he did beautifully and when he walked out of the room I said "Boy, he's great" and we hired him right away.'

John Wells' recollection of Clooney's reading is a little different from the actor's. Wells remembers Clooney having memorised an entire scene from the pilot in which his character confronts a lawyer who has been abusing a child. Wells remembers that Clooney nailed the audition and walked away with the part. Clooney, on the other hand, insists: 'I read the part of Mark Greene. Doug Ross only had four or five scenes in the pilot; there wasn't that much to do in it. But it was a great part. There wasn't really a pilot available at the time. We just read for the best parts.'

Whether he read for Mark Greene or Doug Ross is slightly academic now. The fact is that Clooney impressed Wells and Holcomb and walked away with the role of his career.

'George Clooney and the Doug Ross character seemed like a complete fit,' says casting director John Levey. 'If you're going to cast a character with behaviour that people don't approve of – such as drinking too much and cheating on his girlfriends – you need someone who balances that behaviour with their innate charm and attractiveness. George is one of those people who can get away with pretty much anything because he is so adorable.'

Doug Ross is a deeply flawed and extremely enigmatic character. He has the morals of a rattlesnake. He drinks too much, he sleeps around, he seems determined to lose himself in the moment with almost any woman he can find. But that external behaviour masks a man who is potentially the most intriguing character in the show. Why would a man like Doug Ross want to be a doctor? How does he manage to show enough application to get through medical school? And after all that, why stay in public medicine in as demanding and heart-breaking a speciality as paediatrics? What, the audience is entitled to wonder, is Doug Ross punishing himself for? For what heinous imagined wrong is he trying to atone?

The opportunity to answer even a few of these questions in a long-running series is a prospect which would have most actors drooling. George Clooney is no exception and he seized the chance with both hands. 'I like the flaws in this guy,' says Clooney of Doug Ross. 'I have always been a bit of a hack you know. I've been good in some things and really bad in some things. It's not like people considered me this wonderful television actor. I have always done fine but this is the show that got me out of that,' he says gratefully of *ER*.

Clooney was also able to draw from his own family experiences as far as Doug Ross's drinking was concerned. 'I fashioned the drunk stuff after Uncle George,' explains Clooney. 'Al Pacino did a perfect impression of my Uncle George in *Scent of a Woman*. So now I have to do a mellower one otherwise people accuse me of copying Pacino.'

Although *ER* is an ensemble show with a central core of six, there is no doubt that the show really revolves around two characters – Doug Ross and Mark Greene. They are the yin and yang of the emergency room. Ross is apparently superficial and amoral; Greene is the embodiment of traditional values. Greene is a straight shooter and the moral centre of the show. All the other characters take their lead and are, to a large extent, defined by their reaction to either Greene or Ross. That being the case, the casting of Mark Greene would require as much care as the casting of Doug Ross.

Having got Clooney in place as Ross, it needed someone who would make a good fit as Greene. He would have to be about the same age, less obviously good-looking, but with the sort of skill and dedication which would inspire admiration from Ross. Greene and Ross would have to be friends and Greene would have to have the understanding to see past Ross's shortcomings to recognise his skills as a doctor.

John Wells' first choice for the part of Mark Greene was Anthony Edwards, an actor who had shone in supporting roles in films like *Top Gun* and *The Client*. He was the perfect foil for Tom Cruise and Susan Sarandon in those films but he was unlikely ever to be able to carry a movie on his own. Edwards was unfortunately not available for the pilot because of his own plans to make his directing debut in a small picture. Other actors were tested and read but no one really fitted the bill. In the end, however, Edwards' own film was delayed for a week. This gave him time to come in, read for the network, shoot his scenes and be away again in just seven days. He gave, by all accounts, a remarkable performance and the role was his.

The casting of Susan Lewis was similarly fraught. Sherry Stringfield again seemed the obvious candidate but she was tied up on the Steven Bochco show *NYPD Blue*, where she played the ex-wife of David Caruso's detective John Kelly. Wells and Levey had considered Stringfield for a previous project and were keen to have her for *ER*. They assumed she was tied up but her agent had let it be known that he didn't think her role in *NYPD Blue* would continue. With a little patience on Wells' part and some good grace on the part of Bochco in releasing her from her contract, Stringfield finally became available.

By the standards of Stringfield and Edwards, the casting of Noah Wyle as John Carter went relatively smoothly. Wyle had had small parts in the movies *A Few Good Men* and *Swing Time* and impressed Wells with his ability to play vulnerable without looking stupid. Casting his mentor Peter Benton was again troublesome. Levey and Warner Brothers head of casting Barbara Miller had looked at all sorts of actors without success. They had not yet considered Eriq La Salle because he was busy working on another pilot. But by the time they started filming the pilot the role still hadn't been cast and the shooting schedule was hastily re-arranged to accommodate the lack of a Benton.

Filming began on the Tuesday. La Salle was seen that day, approved by the network the following day and was thrown into the deep end the following day with a huge single take scene in which Benton walks Carter through the emergency room. It was an incredibly complex scene but La Salle handled it with grace and style.

The final piece of the jigsaw had actually been in place for some time. Julianna Margulies, who played head nurse Carol Hathaway, was cast very early on in the process. Hers is arguably the most important role in the pilot. After seeing her being a caring nurse for the better part of two hours the audience is stunned at the end of the show when she appears to commit suicide by taking an overdose of pills. Margulies was perfectly cast as Hathaway but there was some doubt both in her mind and the minds of John Wells and Michael Crichton whether she would make it past the pilot.

With the cast finally in place – there were another 85 speaking parts to cast as well as this central half dozen – shooting of the pilot went ahead. It was essentially the same concept which Crichton had thought of all those

★ *Pin-up doc: George Clooney as Dr Doug Ross.*

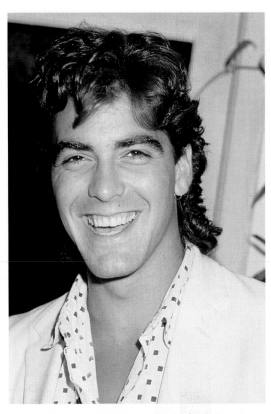

★ Look at that hair! Clooney as a
young actor in The Facts of Life.

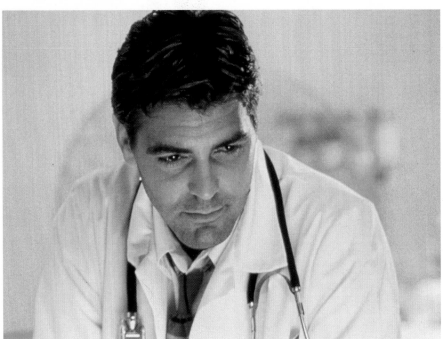

★ George Clooney in pensive mood
as paediatrician Douglas Ross.

★ The principal cast of ER (front) George Clooney,
Julianna Marguilies; (middle) Gloria Reuben, Sherry Stringfield,
Anthony Edwards; (back) Eriq La Salle, Noah Wyle.

★ Noah Wyle and George Clooney
share a tender moment off set!

★ A frosty start: Mae Whitman,
George Clooney, Michelle Pfeiffer
and Alex Linz in One Fine Day.

★ Geroge Clooney and
MTV presenter
Karen Duffy at the
1995 MTV awards.

★ George Clooney with Celine Balitran, and Anthony
Edwards and his wife at the 48th Emmy awards.

★ Michelle Pfeiffer and George Clooney; two single parents coming together in One Fine Day.

★ Clooney as Colonel Thomas Devoe on the set of DreamWorks' The Peacemaker.

★ Clooney and Pfeiffer with their on-screen children in One Fine Day.

★ George Clooney as Bruce Wayne and Uma Thurman as Pamela Isley in Batman and Robin.

★ *George in the Bat suit.*

years ago in *Five Patients* – a day in the life of an emergency room – only now the doctors and nurses involved had names and faces.

'The pilot was about a day in an emergency room,' says Rod Holcomb. 'It was very plain and simple. It defined premises, it defined parameters, it defined how people had to exist within that framework. People came and went and not all the stories were finished because in real life you're not always going to be there to see how something finishes up. But we gave the audience a taste of something real. That was the mission and I think we accomplished it.'

Filming a pilot is just the first step in a network's commitment to the expensive gamble of putting a television series on air. Once a pilot is finished it then has to go through a rigorous period of scrutiny by network number crunchers. Before it ever gets to air – if indeed it does because many pilots are commissioned but few are chosen – the show is watched by carefully selected focus groups who are then intensively questioned by market researchers about what they liked and disliked about the show. This data is then processed and presented to the network in the form of a score which determines whether the show will be picked up or not.

Once this process was completed and the numbers were in, *ER* finished up with one of the highest approval ratings of any drama show on television in living memory. Michael Crichton's observations as a fourth year medical student were finally about to become a series which would change the television landscape for ever.

Chapter 16:
'My Career Just
Got Made'

The pilot episode of *ER* was, given the time which had elapsed since its conception, still remarkably close to the spirit of Crichton's *Five Patients*. Indeed one of the key incidents in the book, a scaffolding collapse which injures several building workers, is still a key element in the pilot.

The first two-hour episode was called *24 Hours*, in recognition presumably of Crichton's intention to show 24 hours in the life of an emergency room. The hustle and bustle of the period, the peaks and troughs of activity, were perfectly charted from start to finish. And no one can doubt George Clooney's ability to get himself noticed. Doug Ross was the first patient to be treated in what would quickly become television's most famous emergency room.

The focus for the pilot is actually Anthony Edwards as Dr Mark Greene as he pulls one of many 18-hour shifts. The programme begins with Greene being roused from sleep in one of the emergency room cubicles. He has been called to deal with a patient who will require his particular skills and cannot be seen by anyone else. The patient turns out to be the resident paediatrician Dr Doug Ross who has turned up at the hospital after a night on the tiles. The audience is first introduced to George Clooney as Doug Ross with the unappealing sight of him lurching unsteadily, obviously the worse for drink, and singing *Danny Boy* off key as he stumbles through the ward giving his best impression of Uncle George. Greene gives Ross some aspirin and dextrose and leaves him to sleep it off in another cubicle. It is obvious to the audience that Ross has a drinking problem and that he is well used to doing this on his nights off. It is also implied that Greene is well used to treating him.

Although he was the first patient into the *ER*, Doug Ross is simply the first of many. All told, Ross included, there are 30 patients dealt with in the opening episode. Finally at the end of his 18-hour shift, the show ends as it had begun with Mark Greene asleep in an examination cubicle.

The pilot may have posted some of the most impressive numbers anyone had ever seen from focus groups but it was still not all plain sailing. The reaction from NBC had not been quite what the people at Amblin were expecting. 'We were expecting an enormous "Jesus, that's great. Let's go,"' says Tony Thomopoulos. 'We didn't get that. At first we got mixed reactions. NBC's concerns were with the non-traditional storytelling.'

By a marvellous irony the very thing that had attracted people like George Clooney, John Wells and even Steven Spielberg himself to the project was the very thing which was now giving NBC pause for second thoughts. The show could still be cancelled. No one had seen it outside of the focus groups and by this stage it would be just another show which didn't make it.

Traditionally television drama had operated on the principles of plot and sub-plot; an 'A' story and a 'B' story. *Hill Street Blues* had broken the mould somewhat by introducing a 'C' storyline and occasionally a 'D' story-line. With *ER*, they were taking the shards of the mould left after *Hill Street* and grinding them into dust. Wells and Crichton were rewriting the rules for American television drama. The pilot had a storyline which went from 'A' to 'Z'. There were at least 20 separate plots weaving in and out of the first episode; there was also impossibly complex and occasionally impenetrable medical jargon and there was as much blood as there was on an abattoir floor.

In addition NBC were also still a little cautious in the wake of their experiences with *Homicide: Life on the Streets*. The Baltimore-based cop show had eventually crept into the bottom of the top twenty – opening the door for shows like *ER* – but it had been a long and hard struggle to get there.

In the end the one thing that saved *ER*, more than anything else, was the quality of talent associated with it. NBC may have had their reservations but you don't commission a pilot from Steven Spielberg and Michael Crichton and then ask them to take it back and do it again. To their credit NBC bit the bullet and did not interfere. The pilot would go out as it had been shot. More than that, when NBC announced their 1994-5 season line-up, it was obvious just how much faith they were placing in their new show. *ER* was to get the jewel in NBC's scheduling crown – Thursday night at ten.

This was a clear signal to the rest of the industry and to the media that

NBC believed the show was a winner. George Clooney for one was delighted. 'The minute we got picked up for Thursday night at ten o'clock I called all my friends,' he says. 'That's because I know television – I grew up in television – and I called all my friends and said "My career just got made." I knew the minute we got Thursday night at ten on NBC.'

There was no doubt either from the schedules or the network's bullish demeanour that *ER* was to be NBC's flagship programme for the coming season. 'The ultimate answer to what NBC felt about *ER* is in that placement,' says Warren Littlefield, the president of the network's entertainment division. 'We have a tradition in that slot which is nearly sacred – *Hill Street Blues*, *LA Law* – and we don't take that pact lightly.'

The pilot episode of *ER* went out on Monday September 19, 1994. The first hour-long episode went out three days later on that Thursday ten o'clock slot on September 22. Within a month it was obvious that the show was the runaway hit of the season, it was a ratings steamroller. The promise of the focus groups had been fulfilled. The shows ratings started unbelievably high and continued to get higher and higher.

'Right around the third weekend we knew we had a job for a while because we went up again and again and again,' says George Clooney. 'When we had about nine shows in the can and they picked us up for the full total of the 26 hours in the season we all thought "Okay, we can start spending some money now."'

Clooney knew that he finally had the bust-out hit that he had been looking for but he did not let it go to his head. The highs and lows his father and aunt had suffered and the natural restraint of his small town childhood came into play again. He wasn't about to spend the money on fast cars and faster women. 'I'm smarter about money,' he says. 'Or at least I have some sense that maybe I won't blow everything. I mean it's a case of "Let's leave a little over here so that we don't end up in a trailer."' On the subject of women, incidentally, Clooney had gone back on his pledge never to be involved with actresses again after his divorce from Talia Balsam. He was now dating another actress, Kimberley Russell, star of the ABC sitcom *Head of the Class* and former girlfriend of Eddie Murphy.

Clooney had been looking for his place in the spotlight all his life and now it had arrived. With hindsight, in a recent interview, he admitted that the wait had been good for him. 'I remember when I was doing *The Facts of Life* and I was 24 years old,' he recalls. 'Somebody would say "You're great", which I wasn't. I would believe them. I kind of bought it. I hate to think what I would have done if I'd actually been any good, or on a good show, or in a big movie. I would have been a nightmare.'

Of his current younger co-stars, he says: 'These guys are great, Noah Wyle handles it so well. I don't think I would have been prepared for it at his age.'

The executive producer of *ER*, John Wells, had been one of Clooney's greatest supporters. He had always believed that the actor's looks got in the way of his talent and he had never been tested dramatically. Finally with Doug Ross, George Clooney had found a role which would exploit both his looks and his ability. Although he only featured in a few scenes in the pilot he was required to display more range in those scenes than he had been required to show in his whole career to date.

To begin with we see him as a drunk and a man who has his problems. In his next scene, the following day, he is shown as a team player and a gifted physician as he steps in to help an old woman who goes into cardiac arrest while he is examining her for unexplained abdominal pain. Later he has the opportunity to show his bedside manner when he helps a young student doctor to calm a small boy and his anxious mother. Ross also intuitively diagnoses the boy as the first eight-year-old ulcer victim he's ever seen. In between times Ross has also been exposed as a Lothario as he tries to hit on the young student doctor and also engages in a laddish conversation with Mark Greene in which he tries to get Greene to admit he has been unfaithful to his wife.

However, his most dramatic moment, and the scene which redeems Doug Ross as a character in the eyes of the viewing millions, comes when he has to deal with his final patient. A baby boy has been brought in by his babysitter because he won't stop crying. The distraught girl tells Ross that the baby's mother said the infant had fallen out of its cot earlier that afternoon. Ross is concerned when he examines the child and discovers clear evidence of old bruising, a fractured skull and what appear to be cigarette burns.

Ross confronts the child's mother with the evidence when she arrives at the emergency room. He tells her that in his opinion the child has been abused and that she ought to get herself an attorney. He is visibly shocked when she tells him that she is an attorney. Ross comes close to losing control and yells at the mother, asking how she can do that to a child. The scene ends with Ross calling the social welfare authorities and leaving the examination room in a disgusted rage.

This is the scene which John Wells recalls Clooney reading at an early audition. Clooney had memorised the whole scene and played it with breathtaking intensity. The effect on screen is similarly compelling. The audience can barely look away as the man they saw at the start of the show as a hopeless, drunken fool turns into a champion of a patient who cannot speak for himself. It is a marvellous piece of television acting and this scene alone probably established George Clooney as a major player the moment anyone saw it.

There is no doubt that Doug Ross is the most appealing character in the show both from the point of view of the actor and the audience. He is the one whose character is revealed piecemeal, and continues to be revealed in the three seasons of the show so far. It is a character into which an actor can grow and Clooney continues to expand the audience's understanding of Doug Ross. His own view of his television alter ego is deceptively simple.

'Doug Ross is a guy in his mid-thirties who has just discovered,' explains Clooney, 'that all the things he used to do in life – partying a little too hard and chasing the girls a little too much – are all starting to catch up to him. It's not working like it used to. He is faced with having to deal with his inadequacies as an adult.'

It would not be stretching the imagination too much to suggest that what we are seeing Clooney portraying on screen is the process he had recently had to come to terms with in his own life. His own period at the end of his twenties when, by his own admission, he lost control sound very similar to the realisation which Doug Ross is slowly having to accept. Ross is a man who has clearly had to endure a great deal of emotional pain in his life. It is this perhaps which enables him to empathise so much with his young patients, many of them too young to articulate their own pain. It would not be unreasonable to suggest that with the recent break-up of a marriage, the death of a man he loved dearly and the near collapse of his career, Clooney has brought at least a little of that pain to Doug Ross.

Clooney would deny this. He claims he is not a method actor. But he is an intelligent man and he must realise that, consciously or unconsciously, his own experience informs the role that he plays. No matter what anyone else might suggest in interviews or feature profiles, Clooney adamantly maintains that the role is not autobiographical. 'The alcoholic thing is funny because I can drink with the best of them,' he says, commenting on one aspect of Doug Ross's character. 'But I'm not even in the same league as most of my family members. And almost everyone in my family, at one time or another, has been a drug addict or an alcoholic. I want the alcohol part of Doug Ross to become a real problem because, as an actor, that's great stuff to do.'

His interest in emulating Doug Ross, however, is confined to those moments when he is actually on the set of *ER*. 'We both live hard,' says Clooney conceding one obvious and undeniable parallel, 'but he's a sad figure and I've had a great life.'

Chapter 17:
Doug and Carol

The pilot show for *ER* was a resounding success. It attracted the sort of audiences which the advance research suggested it would and it broke new ground in the way it told its story. But it also broke new ground in the way it dealt with the characters.

When the first episode of *ER* proper went on air three days after the pilot, one of the cast members was missing. Nurse Carol Hathaway had apparently been killed off in the pilot. Everyone watching the show was stunned when an overdose victim was brought in and it turned out to be Carol Hathaway who had gone off shift a few hours earlier. No one, however, was more stunned than Doug Ross. The show ended with the presumption that the doctors would fail in their attempts to revive her and she would be the show's first high profile casualty.

George Clooney was not entirely happy with the way Julianna Margulies' character was being treated. Hathaway was a large part of Doug Ross's subtext. It was implied that he had broken her heart through his inability to commit and thus he had contributed to her suicide attempt. Hathaway meant a lot to Ross as a character and Clooney as an actor. Clooney also liked the way the two characters had related in the pilot. 'John Wells has made the characters important,' says Clooney, 'because he understands that the audience relates to the story through the characters. The directors contribute in the same way. The Hathaway-Ross love scenario wasn't really in the pilot script at all. Rod Holcomb simply created it by his use of camera angles. Her suicide attempt became personal because the audience saw it through Ross's eyes. The same thing happened with the childbirth scene in the pilot. You watched it through Noah Wyle's eyes as

Carter, the new boy on the set. The writers do a brilliant job with the script and the directors make it even better.'

Clooney very much wanted Julianna Margulies to be a regular on the show. He felt strongly enough to raise it with the network chiefs back at NBC headquarters in New York. 'I went to New York to talk to Don Ohlmeyer, the West Coast president, and Warren Littlefield, the head of entertainment,' recalls Clooney. 'I said "It's too bad Julianna dies." In typical network fashion they then told me "She's not necessarily dead."'

Clooney had in fact crystallised an issue which had been bubbling since the pilot had first been commissioned. Right from the start John Wells and Michael Crichton had wondered if they were doing the right thing by killing her off. 'Hathaway was supposed to die in the pilot,' admits Wells, 'and we really agonised about it because it seemed like very much a television convention to have her not die. In serious television, however, when you have a wonderful actress who delivers great material for you, you swallow hard and get over the story problems. In the pilot she is medically dead, everything that is said about her points in that direction. But Julianna was so wonderful that Michael and I decided "Okay, we'll strain the plausibility in this case and keep Hathaway alive and just have her recover fast." Julianna is a wonderful actress and we were really lucky to get her.'

So, thanks to George Clooney, Carol Hathaway lived to nurse another day. In fact she returned by the second episode of the series proper with a memorable opening line. 'I'm here to unload that new shipment of barbiturates,' she said as she arrived for work.

Clooney was pleased with his victory and the moment he left the NBC offices he called Margulies to let her know that the prognosis for her character had just improved exponentially. 'He called me just in time,' recalls Margulies. 'I was just about to cut my hair, dye it red and straighten it for a different job.'

Carol Hathaway's miraculous resurrection is the only time that *ER* has stooped to such obvious expediency in its three seasons. But the Hathaway situation also subtly indicated where the power lay on the show. There was no doubt that George Clooney was the man with the clout. Clooney of course was the television veteran and, slowly but surely, he became the spokesman for the show. He was an old hand at television. Watching him walk around the Warners set was, by all accounts, like watching him wander through his personal fiefdom.

NBC was smart enough to cash in on that. Clooney was the attractive and acceptable face of *ER* and he was the one who acted as point man on the chat shows and the various other promotional appearances. He was the one who was hand-picked by the network potentates to go on *The Tonight Show* with Jay Leno on the Friday night before the pilot. He was the one who would convince Leno's people, the audience NBC desperately wanted, that they should tune in to his show on the Monday.

Clooney's debut performance on *The Tonight Show* was a televisual tour de force. Although Jay Leno was lagging behind the hipper David Letterman in the ratings at that point, his audience was perceived to be more mainstream. Clooney came on and charmed them like the veteran television performer that he was. What did it matter that this was one of the biggest shows in the country, he'd been doing this sort of thing since he was in short trousers. It could also not have failed to register that this was the show that Leno had inherited from Johnny Carson. This was the show that George Clooney's own father – like all chat show hosts – aspired to and would have given anything to present.

As part of his bid to schmooze the nation, Clooney also came clean with one of his vintage practical jokes. After the earthquake hit Los Angeles Clooney's house had been damaged and he was sleeping at a friend's house. His friend had a cat and while he was there Clooney decided to be a good guest and cleaned out the litter tray while his friend was at work. Clooney, however, had neglected to mention that he was doing this and after a couple of days his concerned friend confided in him that he thought his cat was sick because it hadn't used the litter box in a couple of days.

Clooney had the audience in the palm of his hand as he continued the story. He decided not to tell his friend what he had been doing, instead he took extra care to make sure every scrap of evidence was cleaned out of the litter tray. His friend meanwhile continued to worry and after about a fortnight took the cat to the vet and returned home with a generous container of feline laxative.

Over the years Clooney has learned that the best gags require patience. But he knew that the time had come for the pay-off. The following day, while his friend was at work, Clooney used the litter tray himself in lieu of the toilet. 'I waited all day for my friend to come home from work,' says Clooney to Leno and an audience who were on the point of collapse with anticipation of the punchline. 'He came in and then I heard him scream "Oh my God! Kitty!!"'

The audience erupted and Leno was almost paralysed with laughter as Clooney got to the punchline. It was a vintage television moment and a moment for George Clooney to savour. He had taken another big step on the road to stardom. He had also showcased himself as a good guy, the sort of fella who can take a joke and the sort of guy you would like to have around. The point is not whether the cat litter story is true – it sounds suspiciously like one of those stories which is that magic category of 'too good to check' – but rather that Clooney had shown how easily he could captivate an audience. They had fun as they watched *The Tonight Show* on Friday night and who knows how many millions tuned to NBC the following Monday night to see the guy who crapped in a cat box.

Clooney's ambassadorial duties for the show also extended to providing advice and guidance to the other members of the cast. People like Anthony Edwards and Sherry Stringfield were experienced actors but they were complete novices when it came to television network politics. George Clooney took it upon himself to provide them with some on the job training in the fine art of the schmooze. This was not an attempt to establish a pecking order, this was simply the sort of Southern decency with which Clooney had been raised.

'George is my personal barometer, he's my guru,' says Noah Wyle who was doing his first television show at the age of 23. That was more or less the same age Clooney had been when he caught a break on *The Facts of Life*, but there was no one there to show him the ropes. Now he was passing on the tricks of the trade to Wyle, who was as much an innocent abroad in television as John Carter was in the emergency room. 'This is the first TV I've really done,' he continues. 'I didn't know what a share point or a rating was but George coaches me in all that. He tells me what to expect. We'll be at a party and he'll say "That guy over there is a big network executive, you should pay attention to him."'

Likewise when it was Julianna Margulies' turn to subject herself to the nationwide exhibition which is *The Tonight Show*, it was Clooney who was there to provide her with all the pointers she needed. 'He helped me hone my gynaecologist story to tell,' Margulies said later. 'I wouldn't have told it without him. I told it, got a big laugh, and was invited back immediately.'

It goes without saying that Clooney by this time had already had the ultimate benediction of a return date on *The Tonight Show*, when he was even more successful than he had been before. He is now on the 'A' list of guests for every talk show in the country.

It's easy to say with hindsight that *ER* was always going to be a winner and George Clooney was going to be a big star. But the facts are different and the show did have a major struggle to get to air. And, in a bizarre television coincidence – especially at a time when hour-long dramas were an endangered species – it found itself going up against another medical series. Television hadn't had a regular medical drama since *St Elsewhere* closed its doors several years before, now it had two. In the Sixties it was *Dr Kildare* and *Ben Casey*; in the Nineties it would be *ER* and *Chicago Hope*.

The odds on two shows being commissioned in the same season set in hospitals in the same city are incalculable. Both shows were excellent in their own right and both would have thrived under almost any circumstances. But in competition to one another something had to give and *Chicago Hope* never really stood a chance.

'I guess it's because people like police and doctor shows,' says Clooney, trying to explain the sudden emergence of two medical series in the same season. 'I think that they are easy, automatic drama. People come in, you have a story and they leave. As opposed, to say, a story set in a family where you have to create a lot of other situations. But when you watch our show, our show will have maybe 40 stories in it which is a different format from shows that had ever been seen before. They used to have just an 'A' story and a 'B' story line. *Chicago Hope* still does that which is great – and smart the way they do it – but it's different. We are two different shows.'

The shows may have been different but there was no doubt which one the audience preferred. Like *ER*, *Chicago Hope* also had an ensemble cast led by established talent like Mandy Patinkin, Hector Elizondo, Adam Arkin and Peter McNicol. The focus of the show, however, was more laid back than *ER*. It tended not to go for the frantic pace of the emergency room and took a more conventional and more cerebral approach to the storylines. The audience appeared to have difficulty telling the casts apart and in the early days of both shows George Clooney would occasionally be stopped in the street and mistaken for Adam Arkin. There is a passing resemblance between the actors but, as far as ratings were concerned, there was no resemblance at all between the shows. It was no contest and *Chicago Hope* was getting creamed in the ratings.

Chicago Hope had great acting, good stories, superb production values and by any normal standards is a great show. The one thing it did not have was a charismatic star of the calibre of George Clooney. Mandy Patinkin and Adam Arkin were *Chicago Hope's* answer to Anthony Edwards and George Clooney; they are both fine actors but they are somewhat lacking in the charisma stakes. For want of a star presence the show might as well have been lost.

Chicago Hope was supposed to go head to head with *ER* but the CBS show was very quickly, and somewhat illogically, moved to nine o'clock on the Thursday night. And when the audience surprisingly did not have the stomach for two hours of medical drama back to back it was then moved to Monday night halfway through the season. Competition between the two shows was so intense that when *Chicago Hope* moved to Monday night, NBC announced an unprecedented re-run of the *ER* pilot on the same night. This was unheard of, to re-run a pilot halfway through a season. CBS were less than pleased. No one, however, was more outraged than *Chicago Hope* star Mandy Patinkin who, on his own initiative, asked for a meeting with NBC executive Don Ohlmeyer at which he proceeded to berate him soundly for pitting the two shows at each other's throats.

ER had effectively killed *Chicago Hope's* chances of being a major hit. By the end of the season, when *ER* would finish in second place in the over-all ratings behind *Seinfeld*, *Chicago Hope* didn't even make the top twenty. However, the rival show would emerge victorious in one final, very important end of season tussle.

The final confirmation that George Clooney had finally become a TV star came halfway through the first season of the show. CBS had already shifted *Chicago Hope* twice, now ABC moved its top-rated news show *Prime Time Live*. The show had been on Thursday at ten for five years. Now it was moving to Wednesday.

The competition had surrendered. Thursday night belonged to *ER*, and the future belonged to George Clooney.

Chapter 18:
Mending Fences

That first season of *ER* also brought with it a very significant personal moment in George Clooney's life. In the episode entitled *The Gift*, which was episode eleven in the series and broadcast just ten days before Christmas 1994, Rosemary Clooney took what would become a recurring role in the series.

Relations between Clooney and his aunt had been somewhat strained for a time after his stay at her home when he first came to Hollywood. He still harboured a deal of resentment over the way she treated him and for her part she felt he had been less than grateful for the hospitality he had received. That had been more than ten years previously and relations had been slowly normalised over the years since then. Her decision to take the role as Mary Kavanaugh – a grandmother suffering from Alzheimer's who wanders through the ward singing Christmas carols, just like Rosemary Clooney – made for poignant television and set the seal on their reconciliation.

Indeed it is hard to find anyone now who is prouder of George Clooney, his own parents excepted, than his aunt Rosemary. 'I've known George since he was a baby,' she told *TV Guide* magazine. 'He's always had a public personality. He wanted that attention even as a little boy. It's so nice now that he's getting it.'

Rosemary says that even when George was living at her house she knew he would make it some day. 'He threw himself into acting,' she remembered. 'He took the lessons. He did the showcases. He did every audition he could. He was always working toward what he has finally achieved – success. He's had that focus always that he was going to be successful. Don't be fooled by that self-deprecating humour,' she cautioned. 'He's always kidding but he's deadly serious. That's why this job on *ER* is so wonderful. He has a chance to do serious things and reveal a side of him that people aren't aware of.'

The role of Doug Ross was giving George Clooney everything he had ever wanted from any part. There was the visibility and the recognition of course, but this was also a part in which he could invest some dramatic weight. Clooney has matured as an actor and grown into the role in a way which even he could hardly have thought possible when he read for the pilot.

And Ross was not confined to the stereotypical womanising drunk audiences had met in that pilot show. The character, in common with all the other characters in the series, was allowed to show its various facets as the series progressed. As Clooney had guessed that it would, the characters were being revealed by the very fragmentary storylines which NBC had been leery about to begin with.

One of the most interesting developments in Doug Ross's character in that first series was his relationship with Diane Leeds, the hospital's Risk Management consultant. The two meet initially in episode thirteen – *Long Day's Journey* – when Ross, trying to take out his frustrations after a bad day, goes out to shoot some hoops on the basketball court. He meets a young boy called Jake Leeds on the court and they play together for a while. Jake is waiting for his mother to finish work and when she comes out Ross goes into action. He makes a tentative pass but she tells him she's heard all about him and turns him down.

Eventually, however, he becomes more friendly with the boy, wins her over and they begin a relationship. It all comes crashing down when Ross reverts to type in the second last episode in the series by going back to an old girlfriend. Diane confronts him, Ross begs for a second chance, but she throws him out.

The Diane Leeds storyline gave Clooney some of his nicest scenes in the whole of the first series. It also contributed a great deal to the Doug Ross character by showing that this was a man who was incapable of finding personal happiness. He would conspire to mess it up even when it was being handed to him on a plate.

Diane Leeds was played by Lisa Zane, a veteran of small roles in several movies and television series. It was her biggest television role to date and, such was Clooney's popularity by this stage, simply by being 'Doug Ross's girlfriend' she started to get stopped in the street herself. 'As far as working with George goes, he was absolutely charming,' says Zane. 'He was very funny, a great storyteller and someone who likes to tell jokes as well as play them on people.'

As well as being the network ambassador and unofficial team leader among the *ER* cast, Clooney was also the head jokester. He had finally found a place where his unique talents would be recognised and encouraged. His weapon of choice was the whoopee cushion and Lisa Zane was one of his most spectacular victims. 'At the end of the year they showed the blooper reel at the wrap party,' recalls Zane. 'There was prank after prank and it was all blamed on George and I was treated to the whoopee cushion when we were filming one particular scene. I thought it was my radio mike because I kept hearing this buzzing noise. 'I didn't know what was going on and I kept making these confusing faces at the director,' she continues. 'I'd lean back in my seat and we'd hear this sound. Then I'd sit bolt upright and people would laugh and I'd do it again. I really inadvertently milked the situation, but it was pretty funny. It was wonderful working with George because he kept the whole set buoyant and giggling.'

Clooney's fondness for the whoopee cushion eventually reached the point where he even acquired a remote-controlled one, the better to achieve his goals of reducing his fellow cast members to helpless laughter whenever the occasion demanded it. And his colleagues seem to appreciate his efforts. 'There are times when you want to say "George, calm down a bit,"' admits Julianna Margulies. 'But every now and then, to look over and see him wearing a urine container on his head just makes you feel a little better about your work.'

George Clooney once told a visiting journalist that each of the retakes caused by his shenanigans cost about $6,000. 'But,' as he added in his own defence, 'funny is funny. You can't put a price on those things.'

Not that anyone at the network was likely to take Clooney to task for his jokes. The cast of *ER* were rapidly becoming like royalty at NBC. As far as NBC was concerned *ER* was the final piece in the ratings jigsaw which would give them total dominance on Thursday nights. With the medical drama following on from *Seinfeld* and *Friends*, NBC was with some justification able to bill the evening as 'Must See TV'. It was a much-needed success for the network which never lost a Thursday evening in the ratings while the show was on the air.

To work out what that means to a network like NBC you only have to look at the advertising rates. In American television the rates are directly related to the ratings of the show – a single point in the ratings can mean a difference measured in millions of dollars of advertising revenue. *ER*'s ratings performance meant that by the end of its first season it was able to command a million dollars a minute in advertising revenue, which means that since the show only actually took about around 50 minutes of its hour long slot, each episode could pull in $10 million from advertisers. By the end of that first season only *Seinfeld* with $1.1 million a minute was able to charge more. As a comparison the advertising rate for *Chicago Hope* was less than half that of *ER* at $490,000 a minute.

The show continued to grow in popularity throughout that first season and all of the core cast became household names. None more so than George Clooney. 'It's not me, it's the show,' he said once dismissively. 'If they had a mannequin on *ER* then the mannequin would be the star. I'm just grateful to be on a show that I'm not embarrassed about.'

Anthony Edwards might be first billed but it was obvious who was getting all the attention. It was Clooney who got the lion's share of the magazine covers and the talk show spots and Clooney who was suddenly being talked up for all sorts of movie roles. There was also the inevitable speculation of professional jealousy among the cast. The rumours were further fuelled by the fact that when a number of the cast made a promotional trip to Europe in their first summer hiatus, Clooney was not with them. 'It's all completely contrived,' said Anthony Edwards of the speculation as he continued a round of interviews in London. 'George is a really sweet man.'

Clooney may well have assumed star status on *ER* but he is professional enough to realise where whatever status he has comes from. Towards the end of the first season, by which time the show was hotter than steam, Clooney bought bicycles for all of the cast members as a thank you gift. As an added grace note he had all of their names engraved on the chain guards. As far as he is concerned there is no question of anyone being more or less important than anyone else on the show and if he is the one who is thrust into the lead position then it is – for Clooney at least – on the basis of being first among equals.

But even in that position he found out that being the point man also meant that you were first in line when the bullets started flying. As the heartthrob with the highest visibility on television in years, Clooney found himself a tabloid target. There would scarcely be a week now when he didn't find himself mentioned in *The National Enquirer*, *The Globe*, *The Star* or any of the other supermarket tabloids.

As the show's fame spread, so too did the tabloid tentacles. At one point it seemed like they had interviewed every living soul in Knoxville, Maysfield and Augusta in the hope of finding some dirt on Clooney. Things became so difficult at one stage that Clooney had to caution his family against speaking to the press. 'I said to my sister "What are you doing?" and she started crying,' Clooney recalled after she had given an interview. His sister Ada has now become a very successful accountant and mother of two young children. 'But of all the people in Hollywood I have the least to worry about being exposed. Oh yeah,' he says, 'we were bad kids. We put a fire-cracker in the mailbox. What are they going to nail me for?' he says in exasperation. 'All my ex-girlfriends are old and married now. God love them all,' he added in mock gratitude.

But there was no getting away from his new found 'Hollywood hunk' tag. Lots of people had thought he was cute before when he appeared on *Sisters* and *Roseanne*, but now he was an official tabloid sex symbol. Aunt Rosemary, for example, had known for a long time, even if George hadn't, how hot a sex symbol her nephew was. '*Sisters* was the big step,' she recalls. 'When he was doing that show I had occasion to call at Senator Ted Kennedy's office in Washington. After I was finished one of the secretaries said "You know, the next time you come to Washington, we'd appreciate it if you could bring George."'

Rosemary Clooney also recalled getting better treatment than she felt she was entitled to expect when she went into hospital a couple of years ago. That too she puts down to her nephew and the sympathetic portrayals he and his colleagues give of hard-pressed hospital staff. 'But George has paid his dues,' Rosemary Clooney continued. 'He used to be the highest paid young actor that nobody in the world knew. But now this "hunk" thing is happening. It's kind of funny. I just don't think of him that way but obviously a lot of other people do.'

Clooney himself can be pragmatic about his sex symbol status. It is something he has had to live with for most of his professional life and it is something he doesn't care too much about. 'That lasts for about five minutes,' he says of being regarded as a heartthrob. 'Then you're like "Who?" That's part of what comes with doing what you do. And then it literally goes away as quickly. People go "Doesn't it bother you when they say hunk?" And you go "Well, at least they're not saying schmuck." So does it bother me,' he asks rhetorically. 'No. It's too bad because sometimes it'll categorise you out of being an actor. But maybe that's where I should be. I don't know. It's not for me to define what people see in me, or like in me, or dislike in me. I've just got to do my job. And if people like it, then I get to keep doing it.'

Clooney wouldn't take much pressing to admit that the tabloid sex symbol tag can be a little wearing. Like the time when he was at dinner with some friends in an up-market Los Angeles restaurant. Among the party was actress Nicollette Sheridan, who at that time was singer Michael Bolton's girlfriend. When she got up to leave, Clooney stood up to give her a hug and the two were instantly illuminated in a blaze of flashguns. Before either knew what had happened they had become a tabloid item. Clooney suffered similarly at the hands of the tabloids in being linked with Cindy Crawford, another supermodel, Vendela, and *Friends* stars Courtney Cox and Lisa Kudrow – he and Noah Wyle had guested on NBC's other big hit show as a couple of doctors in one of the better episodes. 'I met one girl that I kind of liked,' says Clooney without naming the woman, 'and it ended up being a story in the tabloids.'

He tells the story without a trace of self-pity in order to make people aware of the plight he now finds himself in rather than feel sorry for him. To be fair to the media though Clooney had had his share of high profile girlfriends. As well as Kelly Preston, Talia Balsam and his then current girlfriend Kimberley Russell, he had also been romantically involved with Denise Crosby – grand-daughter of Bing and *Star Trek:The Next Generation* sex symbol – and DeDee Pfeiffer, his co-star in *Red Surf*, among others.

But Clooney plays down suggestions of being a womaniser. 'I've had my share of dates over the years and I've gone out with my share of women,' he says. 'But calling me a womaniser is a little tough.'

'I'm single. I'm allowed,' he told another interviewer when the subject came up. 'The problem is kind of the image. As you get older that image isn't as cute any more, not like when you're eighteen and going out with a bunch of girls. When you're forty and you do it, it's kind of sad.'

Given the temperament that he has, Clooney is unlikely to stay serious about anything for too long. He has already, he claims, seen the positive side of his alleged sex symbol status. 'The actresses I get to work with are now saying "George, can we rehearse the love scene one more time?"' he joked. 'The difficult thing is that you have to actually live up to that image when it comes down to it and you drop your pants. But I have a stunt double now,' he deadpans. 'I have a wienie wrangler.'

Chapter 19:
Enter Quentin

Although some people took it to mean that there was a split or disharmony among the *ER* cast when George Clooney ducked out of the European promotional trip in the summer of 1995, there was in fact a very good reason for his absence. George Clooney was making a movie. A big one. With a hot director – in fact with two hot directors. And he had the leading role.

Clooney had never really made any secret of the fact that what he wanted to be more than anything else in the world was a movie star. For years he laboured under the terrible frustration of seeing himself as a big star trapped in the small world of television. But he had now been able to deal with that. Realistically he knew that small parts in movies no one ever saw did not properly constitute a film career. After bottoming out with *Baby Talk* and his divorce from Talia Balsam he had taken a different tack. He would do quality television and the big movie roles would follow.

Certainly *Sisters* and *ER* were two of the highest-quality shows around and sure enough he was able to parlay his television work into a movie career. Although the progression from television star to movie lead is a well-worn career path these days, it is a path fraught with danger. For every success like Bruce Willis or John Travolta – and their progression was by no means smooth – there is a Richard Grieco or a David Caruso. As he approached the end of that first season George Clooney's thoughts were starting to turn to the movies. He had a five-year contract with *ER* and the viewing figures suggested it would run the whole five years if he and NBC wanted it to. That gave him four summer breaks in which to make movies and establish himself.

But even as his thoughts turned in this direction there was a cautionary tale being played out for every actor to see. David Caruso had been the
star of the ground-breaking police series *NYPD Blue*. The show was from
Steven Bochco and it was a natural extension of *Hill Street Blues*, but a good
deal grittier with a roving, hand-held camera which gave it a semi-docu-
mentary feel at times. Caruso was the nominal star of the show as Detective
John Kelly.

After only one season, however, Caruso announced that he was leaving the show to pursue a film career. There were suggestions that Caruso left
in a dispute over salary; there are other suggestions that the whole thing was
orchestrated to allow him to leave the show and pursue a film career. The
irony was that Caruso already had a decent film career as a character actor
with memorable roles opposite Robert De Niro in *Mad Dog and Glory* and
Christopher Walken in *King of New York*. However, this was the chance to
star in two lead roles – the first in a remake of *Kiss of Death*, the second an
erotic thriller called *Jade*. Both films bombed at the box office and Caruso
was left with some very expensive egg on his face.

There are other actors whose careers have taken similar turns but this
mini-drama was unfolding just at the moment when Clooney was considering what would have to be a make or break jump into a movie career. He
had learned from his own experience, as well as the example of people like
Caruso, that there is a right way and a wrong way to do things. With the
memory of *Return of the Killer Tomatoes* and *Grizzly II – The Predator* fresh in
his mind, Clooney was in no hurry just to make a movie for its own sake.
There had been some offers but nothing felt sufficiently right for him to take
the plunge. 'You don't want to come out and say, "Okay, now give me a
million bucks and let me carry a film," the first time out after a hit television series,' he told *GQ* magazine. 'Because then you're Richard Grieco, and
it's gone pretty quickly.'

Grieco was one of the stars of a teen-oriented cop show, *21 Jump
Street*, who made two dreadful flop movies – *Mobsters* and *Teen Agent* – and
is now back doing television. Ironically one of his *Jump Street* co-stars was
Johnny Depp, who has handled the transition from small screen to big
screen much more successfully. 'The secret to surviving is not to go for the
whole ring at once,' Clooney continues. 'You want to come out and do a
good third or fourth lead like Mickey Rourke in *Body Heat*.'

On that basis, and with nothing on the horizon which really grabbed
his attention, Clooney had decided that his first break from *ER* would be
spent on a little well-deserved rest and recreation. He had often joked that

the characters in the show achieved that haggard, drawn look as a consequence of simply not wearing make up and letting their 18-hour day, six-
day weeks do the rest. That was only a slight exaggeration and he definitely
felt that the summer of 1995 would be best spent taking things easy. Other
people had different ideas.

There is no doubt that the hottest name behind the cameras in the
Nineties is Quentin Tarantino. He is that rare breed, a superstar director.
Like Spielberg or Hitchcock his name is recognised even by people who
don't go to the movies. Tarantino is a child of the MTV generation. He and
his cohorts hung out at the video store where he worked – Video Archives
in Manhattan Beach – and spent their days watching and discussing
esoteric and obscure movies. His knowledge of cinema is encyclopaedic, his
chutzpah enormous. To get himself noticed, for example, he claimed to
have acted in Jean-Luc Godard's dreadful version of *King Lear*, banking on
the fact that not enough people would have seen the film to challenge him.
He was proved right for a long time and his *King Lear* appearance stayed on
his filmography until he began getting interviewed by people who had seen
just as many films as he had. In truth his acting experience consisted of little
more than a small part in an episode of *The Golden Girls*.

Nonetheless his debut film *Reservoir Dogs*, followed by the staggering
success of *Pulp Fiction* – which won him an Oscar for Best Original
Screenplay – led him to be hailed as the saviour of the modern cinema. As
a consequence of his success, scripts that had been written by him years ago
were being dusted off and reworked. In addition, Tarantino could do pretty
much what he wanted to and at the start of 1995 one of the things he
wanted to do was direct an episode of *ER*. Tarantino directed the second last
episode of the first series – *Motherhood* – the episode, coincidentally, in
which Doug Ross is finally dumped by Diane Leeds.

Tarantino's episode was as flashy and stylish as everything else he does
but it wasn't an especially memorable episode compared to some of the
others done by the show's regular pool of directors. Nonetheless he had
been impressed by George Clooney, who he remembered from the audition
for *Reservoir Dogs* almost four years previously. They had remained friends
and both had a good time while Tarantino was directing the show.

Tarantino also gave Clooney a touch of his own medicine during filming. When Clooney was between takes, a young woman came up to him and
threw herself into his arms professing undying love. Clooney was stunned
and the more he tried to assure her they had never met, the more insistent
she became. Only when he was at the point of complete exasperation did

she finally take off her disguise. It was actress Rosanna Arquette, who had been put up to the stunt by Tarantino.

Now that he was the hottest thing in the business, one of the other uses to which Tarantino had put his new found clout was in sponsoring protégés. His writing partner Roger Avary, for example, was able to direct his first film *Killing Zoe* under Tarantino's patronage. Likewise Tarantino had earmarked the first script he had ever been paid to write as a movie to be directed by Robert Rodriguez. The 26-year-old Texan had caused a sensation with his debut film *El Mariachi* which he had made for just $7,000. He would go on to remake the movie as *Desperado* with a much bigger budget and a rising star in the shape of Antonio Banderas. But for now Rodriguez was working on that Tarantino script.

It was about two bank-robbing brothers who are forced to go on the run after a robbery goes wrong. One of them is a psychopath, the other is a professional criminal who only resorts to actual violence when there is no other alternative. Once the heist backfires on them, they kidnap a family and force them to take them to the Mexican border in their recreation vehicle. After successfully smuggling themselves across the border they wait in a bizarrely named bar called the Tittie Twister. The bar turns out to be populated by vampires and the brothers and their hostages face a fight for their lives. The title of the movie comes from the unusual licensing hours of the Tittie Twister – *From Dusk Till Dawn*.

Tarantino wanted Rodriguez to direct and he wanted to play one of the Gecko brothers himself – Richard, the psychotic one. For the other brother, Seth, the professional criminal, Tarantino was leaning towards veteran actor Robert Blake. Rodriguez wasn't convinced about Blake and was still looking around for other choices.

Clooney, meanwhile, was still hot on the chat show circuit. He had just been invited as a guest on the hippest chat show on American television, *Politically Incorrect*. Hosted by comedian Bill Maher, this Comedy Central cable show had built up a huge following with its format of taking a disparate mix of guests and allowing them to talk about the most outrageous politically incorrect subjects anyone could think of. Rodriguez was settling down to watch the show when he noticed Clooney as one of the guests. Almost immediately he knew he had found Seth Gecko.

'I was really looking for someone new and fresh,' explains Rodriguez. 'I had been really spoiled by Antonio Banderas in *Desperado* who was up and coming and had not been seen in action films before and I wanted someone else like that. A lot of the names that were being suggested were the sort of guys who had done this sort of thing before, they were $2 million a head, and they didn't bring anything fresh with them. Quentin had shown me some *ER* episodes when he was thinking of directing the show and then a little later I saw him on television on an interview show. He was just sitting back and brooding,' Rodriguez continues. 'After that I saw him at an Academy Awards party and then I saw him on the cover of *US* magazine. I showed the picture to Lawrence Bender, the producer, and told him I thought he looked a little like Quentin. George was coming up to his hiatus at this stage and he had no movie roles lined up. The show was hot but not all TV guys transfer to movies and usually you wait a bit longer before giving someone the lead. He hadn't been offered anything and he was planning on taking the summer off when I offered him the lead and he took it. He knew that the part was such a big change from television. He also knew that he might get a younger audience to go out and see him because that's what it takes to be a success in the movie business.'

Rodriguez had cast Clooney as Seth Gecko largely by instinct. He knew, from Tarantino obviously, that he was a good actor and Tarantino could also attest that he was a good guy. But having cast him Rodriguez didn't go out of his way to see any of Clooney's work in case it spoiled his image.

'Once I met him that solidified my choice,' the director explains. 'I was afraid to see too much of his work because as soon as I saw him I really thought he was exactly what I was looking for, and I thought he could be very big indeed. In these days of $20 million stars I would rather make a new star than have to pay for them later when someone else has discovered them. It's fresh and exciting especially when you see them go on and do great things. George had the right sense of humour. He had the right sensibility,' says Rodriguez. 'He knew that he had been in the business a long time and a lot of it was luck and placement and timing. He didn't want to blow this chance, he was prepared to work very hard for it. He used to joke about it too. He would introduce himself to people on the set by going up and saying "Hi, I'm George Clooney, television actor." He knew what it had been like to be unemployed for a long time, especially now that he was the hot ticket.'

So having planned to take the summer off and maybe find himself a nice third or fourth lead in a movie the following year, Clooney suddenly found himself with the biggest film role of his career. He was starring opposite Quentin Tarantino and being directed by Robert Rodriguez, and the rest of the cast included Harvey Keitel and Juliette Lewis.

'There was no method to the madness,' admits Clooney on his decision to do *From Dusk Till Dawn*. He hadn't been specifically looking for something radically different from *ER*. In fact he hadn't been looking for much of anything at all at that time. 'What I wanted to do was a couple of good scenes in a good film,' he continues. 'That's what I was looking for. I did read for a couple of parts, and was offered a couple of roles, and then there were parts that I wanted to do which just weren't around. But then this came around and they said "Do you want to do it?" and I said yes. These guys can't make bad films,' insists Clooney. 'That's the great thing about Robert and Quentin, they are just so talented.'

Chapter 20: Wild Times at the Tittie Twister

A t last, twelve years after he came to Hollywood, George Clooney had a part in a worthwhile movie. It was the chance finally to break out of being a television star and become a movie actor. But there was a problem. It seemed like there had always been a problem when Clooney and movies were involved and this time was no different.

The shooting schedule of *From Dusk Till Dawn*, which had already been accelerated, was pushed up again. That meant it was going to clash with shooting of *ER*. Clooney found to his dismay that his big movie break and his bread and butter television job were going to film at the same time. 'I didn't think I was ever going to get to do it,' he admits now. 'I didn't think that Warner Brothers would let me out. I was needed for a very, very small part in the first two episodes of series two of *ER*. And I didn't really think I had a leg to stand on. You can't say to them "Look, listen, if I do this film it will really help out the show."'

Actually Clooney found out that's exactly what you can say to them, if you ask the right person. 'John Wells is the executive producer of the show and about the nicest person you could ever meet,' says Clooney with genuine warmth. 'He's written some feature scripts too and he is just really talented. But also, the bottom line is, he's a really nice guy.

'With *From Dusk Till Dawn* I had a meeting with him. I walked in and I said "I'm gonna ask something," and he said "What?" And I said "I've been given an opportunity to work with Quentin Tarantino and Robert Rodriguez and Harvey Keitel and all of these people. But it would require some work on the schedule." I also pointed out that I had only got the chance because of him and because of the show and because of that, if I ouldn't do it then I couldn't do it. But if I could then of course I would love o. And John said "Let me work it out." And he did and he has been nothing but a prince through all of this, which is really nice.'

So, with John Wells' skill on the schedules, George Clooney found himself in the heat and the dust of Mexico filming *From Dusk Till Dawn*. The shoot was scheduled so that the more demanding horror scenes were filmed first so what is, in effect, the second half of the double bill was filmed first. And, once a week, George Clooney would dutifully troop back to Los Angeles to meet his commitment to the show which was finally making a movie career possible.

'I worked four days a week on *ER* and three on the film,' he explains. 'I had to learn my lines while making the two-hour round trip between sets. Luckily driving that old Ford Bronco is like therapy for me. I worked seven days a week for 40 days, finishing at three in the morning sometimes for *From Dusk Till Dawn* and just making it to a 6am call on *ER*. But,' he reasons, 'I figured if I'm going to get a shot, it won't come twice.'

'It wasn't that hard to switch back and forth,' he said afterwards about playing Seth Gecko and Doug Ross simultaneously. 'I think there are actors who are much better actors than I who spend time exploring characters and getting into the characters much more. I don't really do that. I just pick up the script, find out what I'm doing that day and go ahead. So because of that it wasn't that hard to do.'

The movie career, however, meant some changes in his television image. Seth Gecko affects a cool and menacing look topped off with a modified Caesar hairstyle. Doug Ross used to have a neat, but nonetheless wavy, head of hair. Changing hairstyles was out, so was wearing a wig for the duration of *ER*'s second series, so returning audiences saw Doug Ross sporting a new 'do'. The Caesar looked seemed to catch on and before long the male cast of *Friends*, and significant numbers of the male population, were also sporting the look.

Working on *From Dusk Till Dawn* meant that Clooney was renewing his acquaintance with Quentin Tarantino who, as Richard Gecko, was doing his first lead in a major movie. His other appearances had been confined to cameos in other people's movies. They were supposed to be brothers in the movie so Tarantino suggested they spend some time together and 'the Gecko brothers' became something of a fixture, albeit briefly, on the Hollywood hip and happening social scene.

'Where did we go?' asks Clooney rhetorically. 'A couple of nights we went to clubs around town and just drank a couple of beers. We went to the

MTV awards together, but we spent a lot of time together before that because Quentin really wanted to do his homework on this one. He really wanted this to be something he explored and did from the very beginning, and I was willing and happy to do whatever he wanted to do.'

Tarantino also lost no time, during this bonding process, in reminding his new brother how abysmal he had been on his *Reservoir Dogs* audition. 'We were just sitting there,' says Clooney, ' when out of the blue he said "You really blew that audition for *Dogs*." Yeah? Thanks Quentin. But Quentin and I actually became very close. It was a funny thing. We both have this kinetic energy and there is a kind of "manicness" to both of us.'

Clooney's kinetic energy was stretched to the limit as he basically worked three days on *From Dusk Till Dawn* and four days on *ER* to cover his commitments to both shows. During the summer, however, when he was shooting *From Dusk Till Dawn*, Clooney was wakened at 5.30 in the morning with a phone call to tell him that he had been nominated for an Emmy award for his work in *ER*. Most of the major cast members had been nominated and he and co-star Anthony Edwards were in the running for Best Actor in a Dramatic Series. In the end the award was won by Mandy Patinkin of *Chicago Hope*, a small but significant victory for the number two show.

ER was also nominated as Best Drama but lost out to *NYPD Blue*. Even so, the show managed to equal a record by winning eight Emmy wins in its freshman year, just as *Hill Street Blues* had done in its first season back in 1981. Among the *ER* winners were Julianna Margulies for Best Supporting Actress, Mimi Leder as Best Director, and writer and medical adviser Lance Gentile for Best Writing.

Although he is inclined to make light of what he does for a living, Clooney and the rest of the cast must have felt that their Emmy nominations – and in Margulies's case her success – were a vindication of what they were doing. They weren't just running around spouting jargon, they were creating a performance.

'Whatever method you choose to work with is fine,' says Clooney of his acting style. 'Brando would still have been great had he not been a method actor. Actors are good or not good based on their individual talent. If you are in a play, or a good film, you can piece together a performance based on personal history and other elements that add colour to a character. On *ER* we show up every morning and we have about nine pages to shoot. Some of it is about the character, and some of it is a matter of survival. So what you learn to do is tell yourself a story. What is really going on in this scene? What am I trying to do? And you do it very quickly. It just comes like second nature to you. There is a danger of it getting too comfortable after a while and you may have to shake things up, but in general it's a much quicker process than it would be under other circumstances.

'I've done a lot of bad television over the years,' says Clooney. 'And,' he adds self-deprecatingly, 'I've been very bad in a lot of bad television. So I have a pretty good perspective on what we do on *ER*. We are on a tremendous show and I will hold what we do against any actor's job as far as difficulty goes; doing a play for eight performances a week is nothing compared to this. Every single workday is fourteen or fifteen hours long. We speak a language we don't understand – nobody comes to work in the morning knowing what tachycardia means. We have to perform medical procedures as if we were professionals – and we have to do that with 50 extras flying through on a Steadicam shot with no cuts, saying "Super ventricular tachyarrhythmia" – without screwing up. It's an ongoing all day process,' he says, 'and it requires great concentration.'

Even though he had been vindicated as an actor, there was still the problem of how to deal with the fact that he had been nominated when he came to work on *From Dusk Till Dawn* that morning. Clooney need not have worried about anyone showing any unwelcome or embarrassing deference when he got to the set. As he made his way to the trailer he found a note pinned to the door of his trailer. It was from the rest of the cast. It said: 'Dear George, Emmy, Schmemmy.'

So the status quo was restored and they went back to work. Little incidents like the Emmy note were good for morale. So too were George Clooney and Harvey Keitel having water pistol duels throughout the shoot. Keitel is one of the modern masters of the American cinema. His command of his craft is such that he is revered with almost God-like status by many of his peers. George Clooney gave Keitel as much respect as he would give anyone but – just like Uncle George had taught him – he wasn't going to be intimidated by him.

So on the first day of shooting Clooney hung around while Keitel finished a tense scene. There was a moment of silence at the end which was eventually punctuated by Clooney cheerily shouting : 'That was terrific, Harvey. Reminds me of my early work.' Keitel responded with a two-word reply more in keeping with his usual tough-guy characters. But he loved Clooney's irreverence and he soon joined in. Apart from the water pistol fights, Keitel would find old publicity eight by tens of Clooney and beg him to autograph them. 'I don't think I have ever seen Harvey Keitel laugh so

much on a movie set,' says producer Lawrence Bender with genuine aston-
ishment.

Even Robert Rodriguez got involved in Clooney's humour. 'Robert is
always asking me "George, how should you shoot this?"' Clooney said in
mock confidence to a reporter visiting the set. 'And I just tell him "If there
is some way you can just cut to me then I think you've got a movie."

'I'm like the dog in *El Mariachi*,' joked Clooney of Rodriguez's debut
picture. 'When he did *El Mariachi*, Robert didn't have a sound sync camera
so later, after filming, he would have the actors repeat their lines onto a tape
recorder. He also did shots of this dog. And then, every time the voices and
the film would get out of sync, he'd just cut to the dog. In this movie I have
become that dog in a lot of scenes,' laughed Clooney.

'George was a real jokester,' agrees Robert Rodriguez. 'He kept the
whole set laughing, he had Harvey cracking up the whole time. There was a
lot of humour on the set but we needed that because we never wanted to
forget that we were making a movie we wanted people to enjoy. You can get
so bogged down in the mechanics that sometimes you forget what you're
doing.'

Rodriguez and Bender were also keen to encourage others to make
sure that Clooney had to take as much as he was dishing out.

'There was one day when Robert got his own back on him,' remembers Bender. 'We had all these pads out ready for George to do a stunt. He
was doing it himself because the camera was right in his face. So he walked
off to get padded up and there was a pile of cushions about as high as a
table for him to land on. And that's when Robert got everyone together to
play a gag on George. So when George comes back Robert was behind the
lens and he said "You know what, can you just pull that one pad off because
it's in the shot."

'So the stunt guys came in and pulled the one pad off. George is a little
concerned because he's got to fly though the air for about ten feet and land
on his back. but he's saying nothing. Then Robert said "It's still in the shot,
better pull another one off" and the stunt guys came in again and pulled off
another pad. He kept doing that until they were almost all gone. Then he
said "Put a furniture pad on, it'll be all right" and they put this tiny, thin
furniture pad out there.

'George, who had been watching all this quietly, was just on the point
of saying something when everyone else started cracking up. He was trying
to be the tough guy but he was on the point of complaining. And that's
when we let him in on the gag.'

Joking aside, both Clooney and Rodriguez knew they had a job to do. Clooney had to carry a picture for the first time while Rodriguez had to make Clooney into a star. The director joked that he would be sent to movie hell if Clooney didn't make it big after *From Dusk Till Dawn*.

But Rodriguez also knew he could cash in on the fact that Clooney was playing against type. Here was America's favourite paediatrician and he was blowing people away right, left and centre. Rodriguez believed, quite correctly, that combination would be a box office winner. 'Bruce Willis didn't become successful in movies at first because he went out and did *Blind Date*, which was a Blake Edwards comedy,' Rodriguez explained. 'He'd been doing comedy on television for a couple of seasons on *Moonlighting* which people could see for free so why should they pay seven bucks to see him do that in the movies. But once Bruce Willis started doing action movies he became a big star. So George couldn't do more nice guy roles because people can see that on television free, but *From Dusk Till Dawn* is something they would pay to see, to see George be bad.'

If Rodriguez saw his agenda in simple terms, Clooney was having some difficulty in coming to terms with his end of the bargain. He was finding it a little hard to adjust to the different pacing and discipline of a feature film shoot as opposed to the hectic whirl of filming *ER*. He was also having some problems in giving himself over to the director. Years of working on television had left him with an innate distrust of the men behind the camera which he was now struggling to overcome.

'We had fifteen directors on the 26 episodes of *ER* we did in the first year,' he said by way of explanation during a location interview on a break from shooting *From Dusk Till Dawn*. 'Each one of those wants it to be their episode on which Doug Ross cries because that would make it special. Obviously I can't cry in every one.

'They say "Do this" and you say "I got it" and then you do what you do anyway. You come in here,' he says referring to the movie set, 'and it's intimidating to me because you have to pay attention. On *ER* we're shooting about nine pages a day. Our problem is not so much acting as it is trying to get the words out of your mouth accurately in a take. If you screw up you have to start all over again with the extras and eight actors all working at the same time. And it's all about medical stuff so it's easy to screw up.

'I tell you,' said Clooney with a laugh on the Rodriguez set, 'it's a relief to come here and just stick a gun in some guy's mouth and blow the back of his head off.'

Chapter 21:
Enter Quentin
Again

With shooting on *From Dusk Till Dawn* completed, George Clooney could go back to concentrating on playing Doug Ross in *ER*.

Going back on the show there was, perhaps, a trace of resentment in the way it had been dealt with in the Emmy awards. Although it had won eight, it had missed out on the brass ring of Best Drama and Clooney, for one, felt they had been harshly dealt with. He confessed that he was surprised that *NYPD Blue* had been given the nod ahead of them for the coveted award.

'Also,' he said in an interview at the start of the second series, 'Tony Edwards should have won Best Actor. It's as simple as that. He captained the best show on television for a year and he should have won for the performance he gave in *Love's Labors Lost*.'

Love's Labors Lost, the eighteenth episode in series one in which Mark Greene tries and fails to save a pregnant mother after misdiagnosing a complication in childbirth, remains the single best episode in *ER* to date. It is genuine, heart-stopping, compelling drama and ranks with anything American television can offer.

One of the hardest things any show can do is follow a successful debut season. There is enormous pressure to avoid the dreaded sophomore slump which highlights the fact that many popular shows don't have legs. Clooney and everyone else connected with *ER* knew that they were going to be under a lot of scrutiny in the second season to make sure that they were not just a flash in the pan.

The backroom team at *ER* were also taking precautions to maintain the show's high standards. During the summer hiatus Neal Baer, one of the team of writers assigned to the show, compiled an addition to the reference book which serves as the bible for the *ER* staff. The new section was called 'Fourth Year Medical Student' which included all sorts of information based on his own experiences as a medical student. The key cast members – and especially Noah Wyle as John Carter – could digest this to get more insight into their characters. Baer incidentally brought a lot of his own experience to his *ER* scripts. Mary Kavanaugh, the singing Alzheimer's patient played by Rosemary Clooney, came directly from a case he dealt with when he was a student himself.

Even with all this extra preparation George Clooney knew that the second season was going to be a tough one. 'One reason our show took off was because it was about something you hadn't seen before,' he told *TV Guide*. 'But gurneys bashing through doors – that gimmick is old hat now.'

There was the added challenge in the second year of being the show to beat. Although they were the kings of Thursday night, that only meant that they had become a target. In their second year they found themselves going head to head with another heavily touted show, *Murder One*. This was a new series from Steven Bochco for ABC which would follow a single murder case from start to finish over its 26 episodes. '*Murder One* is going to have a very difficult time,' said Clooney turning the conventional wisdom on its head. 'ABC might be the strongest network but Thursday is NBC's night.'

In the end Clooney's assessment proved accurate. *Murder One* got great reviews but it did not entrance audiences the way it enraptured the critics. Its serial nature meant that audiences felt they had to commit to watching all 26 shows and once they missed an episode they didn't go back. Its own ground-breaking structure worked against it but it also failed to cope with an unprecedentedly strong series of *ER* storylines. Clooney felt it was more important in the second series to get involved in the personal lives of the characters rather than simply relying on the drama of the emergency room to hook the audience.

'This is the year where my character starts to figure out that the way he's skated through life doesn't really work any more,' Clooney continued. 'In the seventh episode it comes to a head. I hit rock bottom and I think people will understand all the dumb things I do.'

The episode Clooney referred to, *Hell and High Water*, is one of the outstanding shows in the three seasons of *ER* to date. It was written by Neal Baer and directed by Christopher Chulack, who is also one of the show's producers. And, as Clooney promised, it does offer some sort of explanation for Ross's behaviour. The episode comes at the climax of a story arc which has seen Ross descend further and further into the moral mire. He has clashed with his superiors about what he believes is an overdose which has been prescribed for a sick child; he has betrayed John Carter by sleeping with his girlfriend; he has rowed with his closest friend Mark Greene when he finds out about the affair; and finally he loses his fellowship after another run in with his boss. All of this is set against a backdrop of mysterious phone calls he has been receiving which turn out to be from his estranged father.

Hell and High Water opens with Ross looking for another job and appearing to have found one in a soulless, private health care hospital which will offer a huge amount of money but not much in the way of satisfaction. After the interview he is heading for a date when his plans are interrupted. He comes across a young boy trapped in a storm drain. It's a wet night and the rain is torrential and unremitting. Ross sends the boy's friend for help while he goes into the drain to get him out. It is not as simple as it appears – the boy is trapped and Ross cannot release him on his own. The water continues to rise as the rain continues to pour down. The boy will drown – and Ross might too – if he is not rescued. Ross chooses to stay with the boy, trying to keep his head above water, and as the chill factor increases trying to stop him from dying of hypothermia. They are eventually rescued and Ross commandeers a news helicopter to take them to County General. His life, his reputation and the child's health are all on the line and it is being captured live on camera and beamed out to an anxious city.

Hell and High Water and the next episode, *The Secret Sharer*, do indeed cast a great deal of light on the enigma which is Doug Ross. The boy is saved of course and Ross gets his job back but he is no sooner back at County General than he is fighting with Mark Greene again. As George Clooney promised, this seventh episode and the plot, which spins off into subsequent episodes, does go a long way to explaining what Ross is all about.

The audience is left to surmise that Ross is the way he is because of his relationship with his father. Ray Ross does eventually turn up later in the series, played by James Farentino. It turns out that Ray Ross is a philanderer who left Doug and his mother. Doug grew up with a strong sense of rejection from his own father and with a complete lack of any role model. He is the way he is, we understand, because he knows no better. The lack of a relationship with his father has left him in an emotional vacuum but at the same time his anger and his resentment of his father have dominated his life. The combination has left him unable to sustain any serious emotional relationship. By extension we are also left to understand that his empathy with his young charges is because he does genuinely share their pain and is trying to offer the solace and protection he never had himself as a child.

Of course now that we understand Ross and Ross understands himself that doesn't really do much to change the character. His reconciliation with his father, for example, ends with Ross having a relationship with his father's latest mistress. But by finally confronting his father and dealing with his feelings about him Ross is at least on the road to recovery.

These second series episodes gave Clooney the opportunity he had never had before of stretching himself as an actor. He was allowed to show a range of emotions as Doug Ross tries to deal with his problems and the results are very impressive. His talent combined with some marvellously perceptive writing enabled Clooney to change completely the way the audience looked at Ross to the point where, by the end of series two, he had become one of the most sympathetic characters in the show.

There were other big changes for George Clooney during that second series too. For one thing he had become a bona fide movie star. Nothing in Hollywood is ever a surprise. Information sweeps through the film community like a firestorm and nothing remains secret for very long, especially not a new hot property. Whether it's from the film company itself or from the developing labs or the cutting room or just crew scuttlebutt, the result is an information network which would put the CIA to shame. *From Dusk Till Dawn* wasn't due to be released until January 1996 but the word was out already that George Clooney was hot.

'While he was editing the film, Robert put together a trailer showcasing me, complete with fake reviews,' explains Clooney. Then he sent the tapes around to some agents to get some buzz going. Robert said "All we have to do is send some bootleg footage around town so people will want to see you. You'll be a millionaire before the movie even comes out." Well, it kind of worked,' Clooney continues. 'Studios who wouldn't throw me a bone with a small role before were now calling with some very big offers.'

When he was young George Clooney had wanted to be a baseball player more than anything else. Now that he had followed his other chosen career he found himself living out a baseball analogy. George Clooney had just become the number one draft pick and – just like baseball franchises – he found that the big studios were willing to trade off other properties to get the number one pick.

In November 1995, only weeks after *ER* had started its second series, George Clooney found himself in the big leagues. *From Dusk Till Dawn* had been a big deal for him but in Hollywood terms it was a small picture. The budget was only $12 million and although it was nominally backed by Miramax – the largest and most influential company in the independent sector – it was being handled by Dimension Films, a Miramax subsidiary which allowed the parent company to maintain a discreet distance if it felt it necessary. Now Universal Pictures wanted Clooney.

Comic strip heroes were back in vogue in Hollywood. The *Batman* series had been phenomenally successful and Alec Baldwin had brought *The Shadow* to the big screen that summer, albeit with considerably less success. There were also moves afoot to make a movie based on *The Phantom*. Universal, however, wanted to make a movie based on the radio and television hero *The Green Hornet*.

The Green Hornet was crusading journalist Britt Reid by day and two-fisted superhero by night. Aided by his faithful manservant Kato he battled evil wherever it appeared. Clooney, with his clean-cut good looks and dashing demeanour, was their first choice to play Britt Reid. He was to be teamed up with rising action star Jason Scott Lee as Kato, his martial artist assistant. Ace horror director Sam Raimi was in negotiations to direct the movie, which was to be shot in spring 1996.

Clooney was thrilled to be given the opportunity to star in a major studio movie which might well turn into a successful franchise. He would doubtless have been even more thrilled by the $3 million pay cheque which the part brought with it. It was more money than he had ever earned for a single role in his life and the recognition it brought with it was a stratospheric leap in his career. But within weeks of signing on for *The Green Hornet*, Clooney found himself in the middle of a bidding war with money being thrown at him from all sides.

Steven Spielberg, as he had done many times in a relatively short career, had changed the Hollywood topography once again. This time he did it by setting up his own company, DreamWorks SKG – the company takes its name from the initials of the surnames of its founding partners, Spielberg, former Disney boss Jeffrey Katzenberg, and record industry magnate David Geffen. Between them this triumvirate planned to set up a company which would dominate the entertainment industry into the millennium. Strategic alliances with people like Bill Gates at Microsoft only enhanced that possibility.

But they were all movie people at heart; even Geffen had become a highly successful producer of movies like *Interview with the Vampire*. It was on their movie record that they would first and foremost be judged and they had already ear-marked their first project.

The Peacemaker was the first movie to be given the green light by DreamWorks. It is a post-Cold war nuclear thriller and Spielberg had no doubt about who he wanted for the lead role. He wanted George Clooney. It was important for DreamWorks to get a film into production as quickly as possible and they wanted *The Peacemaker* to shoot in the spring and summer of 1996.

The fact that Clooney was signed to do *The Green Hornet* for Universal was only one of a series of factors which left the studio caught between the proverbial rock and a hard place. For one thing DreamWorks felt they were owed some degree of loyalty by the man who had become a star thanks to the series backed by Steven Spielberg. For another Spielberg had just agreed to direct *The Lost World* for Universal. This was his long-awaited directing comeback after *Schindler's List*, which he had done for Universal. It was also the sequel to his *Jurassic Park*, the most successful film ever made, which Spielberg had also done for Universal.

The combination of all these factors gave Spielberg enough leverage with Universal to get Clooney out of a signed contract for *The Green Hornet*. He would now do *The Peacemaker* instead in the summer of 1996 for a fee which was thought to be a little more than the $3 million he was to get for *The Green Hornet*. There was some consolation for Universal, and not just in the form of the anticipated box office revenue from Spielberg's *The Lost World*. As compensation for losing Clooney, which effectively killed off *The Green Hornet* for the time being, Universal would get the rights to distribute *The Peacemaker* outside the United States with DreamWorks keeping the American rights for themselves.

Once the deal was done Spielberg sent a personal note to Clooney in which he said that *The Peacemaker* was their first choice project at DreamWorks and Clooney was their first choice to do it. 'Right now is the best year of my life,' said Clooney at the end of making *From Dusk Till Dawn*. 'I'm getting a lot of offers. Any film that I want next year, at any studio, and they'll hold the film until I'm ready to do it. The world has changed for me, and that's a great thing. But,' he added with a note of realism, 'next year you can be sure it'll be me asking "Do you want fries with that?"'

Chapter 22:
A Star Is Born

*I*t had been quite some time since any new talent provoked the kind of feeding frenzy which surrounded George Clooney, and it wasn't over yet.

Clooney may have been in reflective mood towards the end of 1995 as he marvelled at the changes that had been wrought in his life in a single year. But there was much more to come. In the first week of the new year he found himself linked with yet another high profile project.

His big Christmas present in 1995 had been an offer from Fox 2000 to star opposite Michelle Pfeiffer in their new movie *One Fine Day*. This was a romantic comedy from Ellen Simon and Terrel Seltzer in which Clooney and Pfeiffer played two diametrically opposite single parents. He is a free-wheeling newspaper columnist, she is a committed career woman. Their lives change when a mix-up over child care arrangements mean they each have to look after the other's children to enable them to get through one of the most important days in their respective careers.

Once again the offer on the table from producer Lynda Obst was $3 million and once again there was a snag. *One Fine Day* was due to start shooting in March, which would be right in the middle of Clooney's schedule for *ER*. Again Clooney went to John Wells and again Wells was willing to accommodate him by reducing his screen time in the remaining episodes of series two. He had already agreed to make changes to the start of series three to allow Clooney to film *The Peacemaker* during the summer, so he must have been getting used to it by now.

The George Clooney situation highlighted a dilemma that a great many television companies were now facing. With so much movie talent now being drawn from television it was hardly reasonable to expect every film company in Hollywood to wait until the brief summer hiatus to shoot its movie. On the other hand no one wanted a repeat of the *NYPD Blue* scenario where a star was lost to the show because of a dispute which could have been resolved by clever scheduling. Other Warner shows, like *Friends*, faced the same problem at the same time. Jennifer Aniston and David Schwimmer were making their big screen debuts in *She's the One* and *The Pallbearer* respectively and both of these shooting schedules cut across the *Friends* schedule.

It was a matter of common sense and pragmatism to allow Clooney whatever leeway he needed to accommodate both choices. He was enjoying the work on *ER* and had no desire to leave the show. The producers for their part must have been able to console themselves with the fact that a big box office name – as Clooney was in the process of becoming – could only further enhance their show's status and increase its drawing power. On the other hand it did mean that Clooney would be working non-stop, seven days a week for long periods and there must have been concern on both sides about how this would affect his health and his performance.

One Fine Day was to be directed by Michael Hoffman who had previously done the period drama *Restoration*, so this urban contemporary romantic comedy was something of a change of pace for him. Michelle Pfeiffer had been locked into the female lead for some time but there was some difficulty in casting her male co-star. The project was first offered to Tom Cruise and when he passed it was then offered to Kevin Costner but he also turned it down. After Cruise and Costner both said no, there was genuine disagreement among the production team about who should play newspaper columnist Jack Taylor. Everyone wanted somebody different until they met Clooney and realised he was perfect for the role.

'He's got a great comic sense and he's sexy,' says Michael Hoffman. 'For some reason that's a very, very rare combination. But he's also got a very lonely quality which I really thought was important to this character. His boyishness is critical to irritate and loosen up Michelle over the course of the movie.'

So in the space of three months George Clooney had been cast and signed up for three major movies, two of which he was definitely going to do. And all of this was before his first picture had even been released.

From Dusk Till Dawn was released in American cinemas on January 19, 1996. It immediately fulfilled all of the promise which director Robert Rodriguez and producer Lawrence Bender believed it had shown right from the start. The film went straight to number one in the box office charts with a $10 million opening weekend. Ten million dollars is a magic number in Hollywood, it is the much sought after 'eight figure opening' which suggests that your film will be a hit. To get a $10 million opening in the dog days of the middle of January is quite an achievement. Much of *From Dusk Till Dawn's* appeal was down to the attraction of seeing George Clooney creating mayhem on the big screen. The film eventually topped out at a respectable $25.8 million in the United States and ended up being placed 60th in the rankings of the 146 major films which were released in the United States in 1996. Those figures meant that – even by the bizarre accounting system which prevails in Hollywood – it had made its money back and was almost in profit. More significantly the film took more money overseas than it did in America. The international gross was a very healthy $33.5 million, which suggested that Clooney's appeal was not just confined to American audiences. Most of that foreign box office would have come on the strength of Clooney's presence in *ER* in international territories.

By the time video revenues were added in, *From Dusk Till Dawn* had made a fraction over $79 million in 1996. That's a very healthy return on an investment of $12 million. It is also a set of figures which strongly suggested that George Clooney certainly had what it took to carry a movie.

Reviews of *From Dusk Till Dawn* were mixed, which further suggests that its box office success derives largely from Clooney. But even though critics were unhappy with the dual storyline and the excesses of the second half of the picture, they were generally unanimous in their praise for Clooney's performance. Leading film reviewer Roger Ebert singled him out for his 'admirable restraint in going along with the craziness without being overwhelmed by it'.

George Clooney had made an impressive major movie debut by any standard. More importantly it had come along at exactly the right time. The one thing Hollywood has been desperately short of recently is young classic leading men. None of the current crop of Hollywood leads fit the description. With the exception of Mel Gibson, who can and has turned his hand to anything, Hollywood's current male leads fall into very rigid categories.

Harrison Ford, Michael Douglas and Robert Redford are getting a little too mature to play convincing romantic leads, Jeff Bridges and Val Kilmer are too intense, while others like Brad Pitt, Keanu Reeves and Johnny Depp are too young and too grungey to take these sort of roles. Arnold Schwarzenegger, Sylvester Stallone, Bruce Willis, Kurt Russell and the rest of the action beefcake stable simply look uncomfortable in anything other than action roles.

Tom Cruise and Kevin Costner passed on *One Fine Day* for very good reasons. The bottom line is that they each knew that they would not have been convincing in it. There is no one in Hollywood at the moment who could play the sort of roles that William Holden, Robert Taylor or even Tyrone Power made their own. Indeed in the recent remake of *Sabrina*, director Sydney Pollack had to go to television to find someone, in the shape of Greg Kinnear, to play the William Holden role.

But in George Clooney, producers and directors had found someone who could play those kind of characters. Someone who, as Michael Hoffman pointed out, could be funny and sexy. It is, as he said, a rare combination and it's hard to think of another actor who shows any sign of being able to carry it off. A notable exception would be Pierce Brosnan – another star with his origins in a television series – and it is no coincidence surely that their big screen careers have taken off almost in tandem.

Lawrence Bender, who was persuaded to go with Clooney in *From Dusk Till Dawn*, puts it very well and very simply. 'It's got a lot to do with the way Robert shoots,' he says of director Robert Rodriguez. 'When he shot Antonio Banderas in *Desperado* for example he turned him into an icon. He mythologised this macho, charismatic figure and George is exactly the same. He has this old-fashioned leading man look like we haven't seen since Steve McQueen.'

His leading lady in *One Fine Day*, Michelle Pfeiffer, also managed to sum up succinctly the reasons why George Clooney had suddenly acquired Hollywood heat. 'He's like watching Cary Grant,' she says simply. 'Men will like him because he is a respectable and viable advocate for their position. And women obviously love him.'

George Clooney had finally arrived in Hollywood. As a rule of thumb most actors will tell you that it takes about ten years to become an overnight success. For Clooney it had taken a little longer. It had taken fourteen years, eight television series and more than a dozen pilots but here he was, at last. He was making $3 million a picture and he was landing roles which had been considered for box office kings like Tom Cruise and Kevin Costner. He was working hard but he was finally reaping the rewards of his efforts.

'The truth of the matter is,' he said recently, 'that I'm afraid that out of laziness I could end up letting a moment pass me by that could actually put me in the position where I can choose. Because that's all I'm trying to do,' he insists, 'get to work with better and better people. I had friends who were very successful. Old men with Academy Awards like my uncle José. There were things that were very important to them, like getting up and saying "I'd like to thank . . ." or the fact that their movie opened. But those are just tiny little moments in your life,' he says thoughtfully. 'You look forward to them for months and then it comes, and then it's gone. So what I've learned is that you have to love the entire process. You have to love auditioning, you have to love going to work, because otherwise it all rushes by.'

No one was more delighted with George Clooney's success than Quentin Tarantino. The two men became very close during the filming of *From Dusk Till Dawn*. When the film opened, and opened big, Tarantino was so excited that he began to talk about other projects they might do together. He even mentioned the possibility of a prequel to *From Dusk Till Dawn* showing the earlier adventures of the Gecko boys. Tarantino believed, and there is no reason to doubt him, that Clooney would agree to it like a shot.

Things change. No matter how keen he might be to do any kind of sequel or prequel to his vampire-action movie, George Clooney was about to get a phone call which would exceed all his wildest dreams. It would also ensure that he would never, ever have to ask anyone whether or not they wanted fries with that.

Chapter 23:
The Bat-phone
Rings

The call which would change George Clooney's life irrevocably came one February morning in 1996. The phone rang at Clooney's home in the Hollywood hills. The man on the other end was Joel Schumacher, one of Hollywood's most respected directors and a man with a track record of unalloyed success. His hit films included *Flatliners, Falling Down, The Client, Batman Forever,* and *A Time to Kill.*

'Hey,' said Schumacher, 'do you want to star in one of the biggest movies of all time and one of the greatest film franchises in the world which will give you a shot at a film career?' Clooney, not even knowing what was on offer and suspecting that it might be a gag, simply said 'Sure Joel. Sure.'

And with that phone call George Clooney became the new screen Batman and with it became unquestionably the hottest actor in Hollywood. All of this was on the strength of a film which had only opened a fortnight ago.

The *Batman* franchise was, as Schumacher suggested, one of the most successful in screen history. The Darknight Detective had made his first appearance in comic books in 1939. Created by Bob Kane he quickly became – along with Superman – a cultural icon. There had been a couple of serials and a camp Sixties movie made to cash in on the success of a television series. Despite this no one had tackled the character in all his psychotic glory until 1989.

Batman is the secret identity of millionaire playboy Bruce Wayne. Psychologically scarred by seeing his parents gunned down in front of him by a mugger, he dedicates his life to fighting crime. He is a driven and trau-matised man who is frequently only marginally less psychotic than the people he hunts down. Tim Burton, who had made dark fantasy his own private Hollywood domain, seemed the perfect director to bring the character to the screen.

Michael Keaton, an actor better known for comedy roles in films like *Night Shift*, *Mr Mom* and Burton's *Beetlejuice*, was the surprise choice for the starring role in the 1989 movie. Nonetheless the film, with Jack Nicholson stealing the limelight as Batman's nemesis the Joker, made more than $250 million in America alone in the summer of 1989.

Naturally there would be a sequel. Three years later along came *Batman Returns*. Keaton again took the lead role but this time the villains were played by Danny De Vito as the Penguin and Michelle Pfeiffer as Catwoman. *Batman Returns* was a much darker affair than *Batman*. There were strong sexual overtones and Pfeiffer's fetish-style Catwoman costume raised a lot of eyebrows among parents who were a little concerned about what their children were seeing at the movies. The concerns and the change of tone were reflected in the box office for *Batman Returns* which, although healthy at $163 million, were down by a third on the first one.

Those figures were impressive and there would be a third film in the series but there would have to be changes. Although films like *Batman* and *Batman Returns* are impressive box-office earners, the real money comes in merchandising and licensing.

No self-respecting summer blockbuster can ever expect to make it without serious deals from fast food chains, toy manufacturers, and breakfast cereal companies. On that score the *Batman* franchise was in trouble. The licensees were unhappy with the dark tone of the second film and made it plain that they would like to see a more customer-friendly Batman. Warner Brothers called the key licensees to a meeting and assured them that yes, there would be a third Batman movie, and no, it would not be as dark and troubled as the second one.

There were other problems with the third movie. Tim Burton was not keen to direct a third although he would remain as executive producer. More importantly to the mass audience who don't know or care who is behind the camera, Batman didn't want to do it either. Michael Keaton was unhappy about a number of things, not least the fact that he was essentially a guest star in his own movie. In both films he had played second banana to some grand guignol villains. He was also unhappy about the size of his pay cheque.

When Jack Nicholson signed on to play the Joker he made it a condition of doing the movie that he got a slice of the merchandising action.

Some estimates maintain that because of that he may have made as much as $50 million from the picture. Keaton got nothing like that. In the second film his deal was improved to the point where he got 10 per cent of the box office gross. But if they wanted him back for the third film then he let it be known they would have to increase that amount and make him more central to the plot.

Keaton had played into Warner Brothers' hands. The studio was looking to revamp the franchise, the director had already said he didn't want to do the next movie and now the star was making similar noises. Warner took the opportunity to overhaul the series completely and they and Keaton parted company.

The new director was to be Joel Schumacher; there was a new writer too in the shape of Akiva Goldsman; and finally there was a new Batman.

Val Kilmer, who had made a name for himself in films like *Top Gun*, *The Doors* and *Tombstone*, came on board as Batman. His teenage sidekick Robin who had been a staple of the comic books would also make his debut in this film. Rising young star Chris O'Donnell was tapped for that role.

The third film, *Batman Forever*, again featured larger than life villains. Two Face, a hideously scarred psychopath, was played by Oscar-winner Tommy Lee Jones. The other villain, the Riddler, a manic character who sets puzzles as clues to his crime, was still uncast. Robin Williams was favourite for the role but he was taking a long time to commit to the film and there was a problem over whether he should get a share of the box office gross. While he was still trying to make up his mind the part was offered to Jim Carrey, a new comedy sensation on the strength of *Ace Ventura, Pet Detective* and *Dumb and Dumber*. Carrey agreed to play the Riddler for a flat fee of $6 million and no profit sharing. The rest of the cast was filled out with Nicole Kidman as the love interest, Dr Chase Meridian, and Drew Barrymore and Debi Mazar as Two-Face's molls.

The combination worked. *Batman Forever* was the lightest, most accessible and most fun movie in the series. It grossed $184 million at the American box office, making it the biggest film of 1995. Kilmer was a very acceptable substitute for Keaton. His character was less obviously troubled and he played up the playboy aspect of the Bruce Wayne side of his character. His Batman was altogether sleeker, more athletic and more dangerous than Keaton's.

Although the film was a huge box office success, and the merchandisers were also thrilled by the new kiddie-friendly Batman, there were persistent reports that all was not well. It was being claimed that it was a troubled set and that Kilmer, who has a reputation for being a difficult actor and prone to argue over creative disputes, had lived up to his reputation. According to the highly respected trade paper *The Hollywood Reporter*, he fired four drivers in three days. The paper also quoted sources suggesting he had been abusive to people on set. Schumacher himself preferred to maintain a dignified and diplomatic silence but did, on at least one occasion, refer to his star going ballistic.

Even so the film had been a success and Warners wanted a sequel, and quickly. There had been three years between each of the first three movies. Warners wanted to put the fourth film, *Batman and Robin*, onto a fast track and have it ready to be the cornerstone of their release schedule for the summer of 1997. The showbusiness bible, *Daily Variety*, reported that all four of the principals – Schumacher, Kilmer, O'Donnell and Goldsman – had made an agreement to do the picture in that time frame.

That agreement was made in the late summer of 1995 and everything appeared to be going normally. The four of them pursued their careers in the meantime – Schumacher and Goldsman worked on *A Time To Kill*, Kilmer did *Heat* and *The Ghost and the Darkness*, and O'Donnell did *The Chamber* and *In Love and War* – with the understanding that they would get back together again in August the following year for a September 1 start date on *Batman and Robin*.

The film industry woke up to a bombshell in the trade papers on Valentine's Day in 1996. 'Holy Bat Development' as *Variety* introed their story in the style of the 1967 TV series. Val Kilmer was heading out of the franchise after just one movie and George Clooney was waiting in the wings to be fitted for the cape and cowl. The industry was stunned by the development. The story occupied the attention of the film industry trade papers for most of the next fortnight and, on the strength of the international popularity of the *Batman* movies, made headlines all around the world. Finally on February 26, *Daily Variety* announced that George Clooney had signed to do Batman and Robin as part of a three-picture deal with Warner Brothers worth between $25 and $28 million. His fee for *Batman and Robin* alone would be $10 million. There was also an option on another *Batman* movie but that was not part of the three-picture deal. This meant that, in essence, Clooney had a four-picture contract with one of the biggest studios in Hollywood.

It was an astonishing development. One of the most successful movie franchises would now have its lead character played by a third actor in only four outings. The only comparison anyone could think of was Alec Baldwin's decision not to continue with the Jack Ryan franchise after *The Hunt for Red October* and hand the role on to Harrison Ford. Behind the casting change lay a tangled web of Hollywood intrigue and deal-making. On February 29 *Variety* announced that Schumacher was leaving his Hollywood agency, CAA – the same agency which represented Kilmer – because, according to the paper, 'he was upset over how CAA co-chairman Rick Nicita handled negotiations for Val Kilmer'.

This lengthy *Variety* story finally managed to piece together how Kilmer had blown the biggest role he had ever had and how George Clooney landed the role of his life.

The convoluted saga began in the autumn of 1995 when Kilmer was in negotiations with Paramount Pictures to star as *The Saint* in a big budget adaptation of the devil-may-care adventurer created by Leslie Charteris. Kilmer was due to be paid $6 million for the part but, according to *Variety*, negotiations between his agent Rick Nicita and Paramount had broken down by the end of December. Bizarrely, even though the negotiations had broken down, Kilmer continued to have a series of meetings with *The Saint* director Philip Noyce and it was alleged that everyone concerned expected the actor to do the picture anyway. Kilmer was offering script suggestions and re-writes were being done to accommodate these.

The Saint was due to start filming on March 27, 1996 and could take up to three months assuming it stayed on schedule. Warner Brothers needed Kilmer as early as August for pre-production on *Batman and Robin*. It was a tight deadline but with a little accommodation on both sides it could be achieved.

No one, however, appeared to have told Paramount that Warners had first call on Kilmer's services for *Batman and Robin*. *Variety* claimed that Paramount only heard that he was contractually obligated elsewhere and would require Warner Brothers clearance to do their picture at the beginning of February. By that stage the studio was six weeks into pre-production and had spent around $10 million on *The Saint*. Paramount were stunned but nowhere near as stunned as Warner Brothers co-chairman Bob Daly who, according to *Variety*, was told by Nicita that 'Kilmer didn't want to do *Batman* because of a problem with Joel Schumacher and he was going to do *The Saint*'.

Both sets of studio heads were apoplectic but tried to make the best out of the situation. Warner, who were in prime position because contractually they had first call on Kilmer, could have moved the start date of

Batman and Robin. Paramount had also agreed to set a definite stop date on *The Saint* so Kilmer would be free for pre-production on *Batman and Robin*. They had also agreed to move the release date so the films would not clash in the vital box office period.

Warners, however, could read the signs and had already started looking round for other options, hence George Clooney's phone call from Joel Schumacher. Clooney desperately wanted the role, which he knew would give him everything he had ever wanted. He spent an anxious ten days of waiting and negotiating before he knew that the role was finally his. Rather poignantly, on the day when it was announced that Clooney had the role, *Variety* also reported that Val Kilmer was waiting to hear about developments in case there were last-minute hitches with Clooney. Warner Brothers still had not released Kilmer from his *Batman and Robin* contract but eventually let him go to do *The Saint* which was released in the spring of 1997.

Kilmer appeared to be trying to play one studio off against the other. *Daily Variety* dubbed him 'the Caped Vacillator'. There were other problems too. He was allegedly insisting on his friend, screenwriter Robert Towne, writing the script even though Schumacher was insisting that it be done by Akiva Goldsman who had done such a good job on *Batman Forever*. Kilmer himself had agreed to Goldsman when all four of them made their pact the previous year to do another *Batman* picture.

It's hard to fathom what would make Kilmer behave in such a manner and shoot himself in the foot so spectacularly. His supporters blame the break-up of his marriage to actress Joanne Whalley. The marriage was in difficulty during filming of *Batman Forever*, they suggest as an explanation for his behaviour there, and by the time of the new movie they couple were divorcing. No matter what the reason, it was a colossal act of career sabotage from which he may not recover for a very long time.

Undoubtedly Joel Schumacher played a large part in the choice of George Clooney for the dual role of Bruce Wayne and Batman. His work in *ER* had convinced him of his ability to play Bruce Wayne, and the second half of *From Dusk Till Dawn* proved that he had the chops to handle the action sequences as Batman.

'George is a very interesting actor,' Schumacher told *Vanity Fair* a few weeks into filming of *Batman and Robin*. 'He is someone who has been around a while. He has been in things which have failed. He had become adjusted to the fact that, whatever his dreams were, they were not going to happen. That strength, and sadness, comes from having lived, and it comes across when he does very intense, complex scenes.'

Clooney also had one other factor in his favour. He was perceived as a team player, a good soldier. He would, possibly as a consequence of believing that his dreams had been dashed, give a thoroughly professional performance in whatever he did. His responsibilities extended beyond that. When Steven Spielberg was showing the media and other interested parties round the proposed site for his DreamWorks studio, Clooney was there. There was no need for him to be there to do a 'meet and greet' but there he was. He is a stand-up guy who was simply doing his part to repay the man who had helped resurrect his dreams.

According to Schumacher, you cannot put a price on that. He has only recently spoken out about the trauma of filming *Batman Forever*. 'I was told from the start that Val was difficult and he wasn't for me on *Batman Forever* until one day when he was going ballistic and I had to go in and tell him to shape up,' says Schumacher. 'Jim Carrey was a gentleman but Tommy Lee Jones was very threatened by him and very condescending and cruel. He was very dismissive. You know what?' Schumacher continued in his interview with *Cinescape* magazine, 'I'm really tired of defending overpaid, over-privileged actors. I don't know why we're protecting these people. Is it because we are so afraid that they won't work with us again? I pray that some of them won't work with me again,' says Schumacher.

Chapter 24:
Casa de Clooney

*I*mmediately after he put the phone down from Joel Schumacher's call, George Clooney called his cousin Miguel Ferrer. 'I called him because his hero growing up was Batman,' explains Clooney. 'We used to sit around making plaster Batman figures and other goofy stuff when we were kids. I said to him "Guess what I'm going to be doing in September? I'm going to be in *Batman*." Miguel said "Oh, that's nice. What are you going to do? Be a helper or something?" I said "No, listen. I'm going to be Batman."'

His cousin was ecstatic for him, as were his parents when he phoned to give them the news. He had gone, in the space of a few months, from an actor who wondered if he would ever make it to a man who now had the world at his feet. It was all a little difficult to take in.

'The truth of the matter is I was offered these three films,' Clooney explains. '*The Peacemaker* came along and I jumped at the chance of working with Steven Spielberg. Then *One Fine Day* came along and we found that I could work out my schedule with *ER* to accommodate that. Then in the middle of all this, Joel Schumacher said "How about playing Batman?" I just couldn't see how you could turn any of those down. They were all good projects and all completely different.'

Having landed the part of Batman was only the beginning. Once again there would have to be accommodations made to his *ER* schedule. Doing *Batman and Robin* on top of *One Fine Day* and *The Peacemaker* would mean that Clooney would start one film in March 1996 and be filming almost constantly until the end of January 1997 as he made three movies back to back. Somewhere in there he would also have to make good on his *ER* commitments.

It is to the credit of both John Wells and the rest of the *ER* staff and Clooney himself that they were able to reach an amicable settlement. Warner Brothers owned both the *Batman* and the *ER* franchises and they were very keen to protect their interests. Clooney likewise was unwilling to do anything which would rock the boat. A series of meetings was held between the film and television divisions to see how both could get the best out of the situation.

The situation was not without precedent. When Michael J. Fox starred in the *Back to the Future* film series, he filmed his comedy show *Family Ties* at the same time. Fox's commitment to the sitcom, it has to be said, was much less than Clooney's was to *ER*.

It was decided early on that the only way to placate both sides would be for Clooney to film seven days a week during the duration of *Batman and Robin*. His commitments to *ER* required five days of shooting per week but Warner Television had said they wouldn't insist on a Monday to Friday shoot. Schumacher was happy to have Clooney available for the weekends on *Batman and Robin*. Fortunately for both sides the film and the television series were both being shot on the Warner lot at Burbank so there was no need to allow for travelling time between locations. In the end, by agreeing to change the shooting schedule for *ER* Clooney was able to get away with doing four days on the show and three days on the movie. From Monday to Thursday he would be Doug Ross, and from Friday to Sunday he would be either Bruce Wayne or Batman depending on what the script required.

Hollywood prefers to see things in terms of winners and losers and there is no doubt that, as far as *Batman and Robin* was concerned, once the dust had settled Clooney was a big winner and Kilmer was a serious loser.

'Kilmer really wanted it,' said one source quoted in the *Los Angeles Times* on February 24. 'His agents won't admit it but they played their cards the wrong way. In a friendly way, scheduling can be worked out. But if you make demands people will say "Don't threaten me" and threaten you back. If you are nice everybody likes you.'

In the same paper three days later the doyenne of gossip columnists, Liz Smith, quoted another unnamed source who laid the blame at Kilmer's door, claiming that it was Warner Brothers who had made him a star in *Batman Forever*. 'Not a shred of gratitude came from him,' says Smith's column. 'He is a very destructive guy and his name has never yet opened a film all on its own. But he could have made both *Batman and Robin* and *The Saint* if only he'd behaved better and made an effort to work out some reasonable compromise.'

Smith herself suggested that in some quarters Kilmer was being seen as a David throwing a rock at a wicked Goliath. If that was the case, she said, Warner Brothers had dodged the stone with perfect agility.

And while Kilmer had lost out, good soldier George, the man who would never cause trouble for anyone, had grabbed the brass ring. In landing the part of Batman, George Clooney was about to discover that his life was no longer his own. The media attention which he had got as Doug Ross paled into insignificance compared to the attention which would follow him now as Batman. His every move was deemed to be newsworthy and everyone, or so it seemed, wanted a piece of him.

Clooney had already had some unfortunate brushes with the down side of fame. On the first season of *ER*, just at the point where he had become a household name, he was doing a complicated scene when an extra kept talking and distracting him. Clooney asked her to stop twice and when she didn't he then told her, firmly, "You can't do that." Clooney completed the scene and thought nothing more of it until a few days later when he was served with a writ alleging defamation. The extra, a black woman, had claimed that Clooney made a racist comment. 'She claimed I stood around the set in front of thirty blacks, including the ones I work with and am very close to,' Clooney told *Premiere* magazine, 'and said "Let's go coon hunting some niggers." And when I saw this I thought to myself "Okay, here comes the hell."'

Nothing came of the accusation, which was ultimately dropped. It's almost inconceivable to think of Clooney, who had been raised in a tradition of courtliness by his parents and Uncle George – and who was at that point himself dating a black actress – saying anything so grossly offensive.

The point had been made, however. The 'hell', as he called it, had started and it would not go away any time soon. Indeed with *Batman and Robin* it became even worse. There wasn't a tabloid in the world that wouldn't pay big money for an incriminating George Clooney story. George Clooney was now fair game for anyone with a camera.

He didn't try to duck his responsibilities. He continued to lead as normal a life as possible. He simply withdrew a little and took care to surround himself with people he could trust. One of his admirable qualities is his fierce loyalty. He had remained close to those who had helped him when he came to Los Angeles in 1982 and it was to them he turned once again.

When Clooney moved to Los Angeles and was thrown out of his aunt Rosemary's house he moved in with Tom Matthews and slept in his cupboard. Now Tom Matthews lives with George Clooney. Clooney's retreat from the pressures of Hollywood and the prying lenses of the paparazzi is an eight-bedroomed Tudor-style mansion in the Hollywood Hills. He jokingly refers to it as 'Casa de Clooney' and there is a crude hand-lettered sign identifying it as such. This is where Clooney comes to be a guy, to hang out and to let himself go. Matthews shares the house with Clooney, so does another friend, Matt Adler. Like Clooney they are divorcees who have been crashed and burned in the lottery of love. There is a black Chinese dragon sculpture in one of the living rooms on which all three of them have hung their wedding rings as permanent reminders.

Clooney describes the living arrangements as a sort of training for freedom programme. He once jokingly referred to it as being similar to the movie *Free Willy*, in which the guys are catching their breath and getting their bearings before being returned to the wild.

Casa de Clooney is very definitely a testosterone-rich zone. This is a man's house and it couldn't be mistaken for anything else. There's a pool and a tennis court and a basketball court. There's a classic '59 Corvette in the garage along with that old Ford Bronco which shuttled Clooney to and from Mexico when he was filming *From Dusk Till Dawn*. In the driveway there is a Winnebago which is used chiefly for their guys' only once a year golf binge – next to acting, golf is now Clooney's great passion. Also in the driveway is Max, the pot-bellied pig. Clooney is genuinely devoted to the beast, a reminder of his relationship with Kelly Preston, and Max is a little older, a little heavier – he now tips the scales at around 150 pounds – and considerably grouchier. Now that he is older Max has taken to sleeping in Clooney's bedroom, a practice which Kelly Preston allegedly found less than romantic. He is also sadly half-blind now but still acts as an effective deterrent against unwelcome visitors. To complete the security arrangements, there is an electronic gate through which visitors have to be buzzed in at the end of the drive, and there are fitted sheets over the windows to thwart the attentions of even the longest-lensed stalkerazzi.

The house was badly damaged in the last major Los Angeles earthquake and the rear of the building has now been renewed to the tune of almost a quarter of a million pounds. It's an ill wind which blows no one any good, however, and even the quake was turned into Clooney's advantage as a talk-show anecdote.

'Max was in bed with me and woke up minutes before it happened,' says Clooney. 'And I was about to yell at him for waking me up when suddenly everything just exploded. So I'm naked with Max and running, because the house is on a hill, and if it's going down then I want to be up on the street, dodging the next house. One of my buddies who lives in the downstairs guest house comes running up. He's naked too but he's carrying a gun because he thinks someone is trying to break in. All the while I'm thinking about writing a note to my folks trying to explain that, in case we die, it's not what it seems: two naked men, a gun and a pig.'

But even if the house is not quite what you would expect from Hollywood's hottest property, and the lifestyle is a little unconventional too, this is where Clooney goes to be himself. This is where people see the real George Clooney, as much as such a creation exists.

'I don't know,' said Clooney when he was asked about 'the real George Clooney' recently. 'It's funny. It depends on where you are and when you're there as to what people think of me. When I was doing the show *The Facts of Life*, I was the all-American boy. It changes quickly. The truth is that you get labelled for the character you play. People will talk about Doug Ross being a drunk and a womaniser because that is what I play on the show. Have I been drunk? You bet. Have I gone out with a few women? Sure, I'm a 36-year-old single male in Hollywood. I've been through some long failed relationships and a failed marriage, a lot of which was my fault. If you are single and moving up the ladder then the focus is on you.'

George Clooney was able to deal with the focus being on him for the time being. Very soon he would decide that enough was enough, but for now he was prepared to accept it as the price of fame. Just as he was prepared to accept the inevitable questions about his future career. He had landed three films, each of them it seemed destined to be more successful than the other. In the light of that, what would happen to *ER*?

Clooney had done the inevitable press junket to promote *From Dusk Till Dawn* and became tired of hearing David Caruso's name. By his own estimate he spent a whole weekend telling more than 50 different journalists he wasn't about to 'do a Caruso' on *ER*. Nonetheless the tabloids were already speculating that he would quit the show but Clooney remained adamant that he would see out his contract, if they wanted him to.

'I've told myself to do the honourable thing and stick with the show and be the good guy,' says Clooney. 'First, I think leaving the show would be a betrayal and people watching would say "Screw you!" if I do that. Secondly I don't want to leave. The funny thing is that I have done so much bad TV for so many years,' he continues. 'To do a good television show is a landing place, not a stepping stone. I honestly never believed that I was going to get a show of the quality of *ER*. I'm thrilled to be doing this. Eighty per cent of everything you do as an actor sucks. If you do a good TV show then you're as lucky as you can be. I wasn't going anywhere but there is always that initial fear that anyone who has any kind of success on television is going to leave, so they do nice things like they treat us nicer than they did a year ago.'

One of the nice things that happened was that, not long after it became apparent that the show was a hit and its stars would be hot properties, Steven Spielberg took the core cast members out to lunch. He clearly could see which way the wind would be blowing and wanted to impress upon them the importance of staying with the show.

'What Steven doesn't know is that there is a difference between being David Caruso and being a member of the *ER* cast,' said Clooney. 'If you leave Steven Bochco what you've basically said is "Screw you" to television. If we leave *ER* then we're dumping on Spielberg and Amblin and Warner Brothers. I think if you do that all of a sudden we'd be saying "Well, where do we go from here?"'

Chapter 25:
One Fine Break

O nce the fuss about playing Batman settled down, or at least as much as it was going to in the fifteen months until the film was going to come out, George Clooney got back to the business at hand and returned to the set of *ER*. He was happy there and really had no intention of leaving but over the next year he would weary of having to profess his loyalty in almost every single interview.

It wasn't long until he once again found himself doing double duty as he finished off *ER* and started work on *One Fine Day*. This was a film which would seem to be the most obvious choice for an actor like Clooney. His role as newspaperman Jack Taylor is an old-fashioned Hollywood role which would be meat and drink to Clark Gable or Cary Grant. Cast opposite him as architect Melanie Parker was Michelle Pfeiffer.

Their two characters are both single parents. Pfeiffer is the responsible, meticulous and possibly a little anal type. Clooney is devil-may-care, slapdash and not yet much more than a big kid himself. Clooney's screwup means the kids miss their planned school day out so Clooney and Pfeiffer are left with the kids on their hands on what turns out to be the biggest day in their respective careers. Thanks to a little creative juggling, they alternate looking after their children with meeting their appointments and by the end of the film they have fallen in love, as everyone knew they would.

'We wanted to do an old-time classic romance movie,' says Clooney. 'That's what we wanted. We wanted a romantic comedy. We sat down at the same time and everybody had different ideas, but they were all romantic comedy. I kept saying "*Adam's Rib*. Tracy and Hepburn,"' he continued. 'We wanted to make the banter quick, everything had to move,' he explains. 'We had to give it a kind of old-fashioned feel because the movie ends in a kiss. It doesn't end in people screwing. So, because of that there had to be some kind of flavour to it.

'You know,' he continues, ' the truth is that romantic comedies don't work most of the time any more. We're not really willing to suspend our disbelief. I didn't know if this film would work or not. For me, personally, it was great because I got to work with a good director and work with Michelle. I just didn't know if the movie would work and I was happy and surprised when it did.'

One Fine Day began its journey to the screen as a particularly harassed day in the life of producer Lynda Obst. As one of Hollywood's most successful producers with hits like *The Fisher King* and *Sleepless in Seattle* to her credit, Obst may appear to have it made. But even that kind of success doesn't necessarily shield you from everyday domestic concerns.

'I was having a spectacularly impossible day, logistically, in which I was trying to do my job and deal with the exigencies of a teenage son,' explains Obst. The difficulty in question being whether or not she could arrange her day to produce a hit movie and also make a PTA meeting. 'My situation, it turned out, was quite similar to that of several of my friends who had their own share of hellacious career/child juggling days. I suddenly realised,' says Obst, 'that the new definition of heroism was simply surviving the day as a single mother.'

Obst took her idea to Michelle Pfeiffer's production company Via Rosa and the idea began to take shape. In the first draft of the script there was no Jack Taylor character. Obst says they began to realise that there were men in the world going through exactly the same experience and they were being sexist by excluding them, so by the second draft the Jack Taylor character appeared. No one could agree on who should play Taylor. The part was offered to Tom Cruise and Kevin Costner and eventually George Clooney's name was put forward.

At this stage director Michael Hoffman genuinely feared that they simply wouldn't find anyone suitable for the role. Although he was America's hottest acting property at this stage, George Clooney was still an unknown quantity to Michael Hoffman, who doesn't watch much television. The *ER* phenomenon was a closed book as far as Hoffman was concerned. But once he met Clooney he was bowled over by his magnetic appeal and watched the chemistry between the actor and Pfeiffer as they read together. 'He has a roguish charm coupled with a really remarkable comic ability,' says Hoffman, who had come around late to what most American television executives had known for years.

Although the script started as a way of making of a point about the trials and travails of working single parents, George Clooney didn't see it that way. When he was offered the part he had just finished a blood and guts thriller for Robert Rodriguez and was still hip-deep in gore on a daily basis in the trauma rooms of County General.

'I'm not always the brightest when it comes to things like that,' says Clooney self-deprecatingly of the issues which the film addresses, albeit superficially. 'Some people can look at a script and figure out exactly what it's going to do but I just look for a good character. This was a really well-written character and they came to me and said "Here's an opportunity to play a single father who's kind of irresponsible but a nice guy. It's a pretty good part and you get to play opposite Michelle Pfeiffer." So basically,' he jokes, 'I paid them for the role. I am surprised at the other issues like single parenting,' Clooney continues. 'I'm not a parent, I just have a pet pig to worry about. Michelle has two kids though who were on the set and there was this family atmosphere so I got a dose of what it could feel like. But really I haven't had the chance to think of the issues, I just thought about the character.'

Clooney's pragmatism gave him a peach of a role which enabled him once again to display another side of his screen persona. Jack Taylor's charming rogue is a good deal lighter than Doug Ross and, at the end of the day, considerably more responsible. For Clooney, acting opposite someone of the calibre of Michelle Pfeiffer also presented a fresh challenge.

'Michelle would take seemingly straightforward scenes and move them to a completely different level,' he says with admiration. 'I'm thinking "Uh-oh, I'm going to get my head handed to me here." You kind of have to step up a little bit and pay attention when you work with someone like Michelle or you can easily get left behind. I was intimidated to say the least by working with her,' he continues. 'Forget that she's a big movie star and she's beautiful. She's also one of my favourite actors and I was worried about holding up my end of the role. But she is really good that way, she will give you the opportunity to stay in scenes with her. That's how good she is and how confident she is. I was just really lucky to get that opportunity.'

There is an easy familiarity between Clooney and Pfeiffer on and off screen. She described him as being a lot like the character he plays: 'A little bit of a dickhead but charming at the same time.'

Clooney is the first to admit that he can, indeed, be a dickhead. 'Oh sure,' he agrees easily, 'that's part of the fun. I'd have to think a little more about what she meant by that but I think I can probably be more of a dickhead than anybody.'

Leaving aside her light-hearted observations about his personality, Michelle Pfeiffer is in no doubt about the quality of George Clooney's performance. 'I had always liked George's work,' she says. 'I hadn't seen everything, the most recent thing I had seen was *ER* so I wasn't sure about the comedy element. But when we read through a couple of scenes together I saw that he had really good comedic timing and he is hysterical in the movie, I thought he was so funny. What is really refreshing about George for me is "what you see is what you get". He doesn't have any false pretences. He's not all hidden, he's not all gloomy. I think I used to be more attracted to what is hidden and now I'm so surprised when people are sort of right out there with who they are. It kind of takes you back a little bit because I don't find that people in general are willing to be that way with people any more.

'George didn't really audition,' she goes on. 'He came in and we talked. I felt I liked him. I thought "This guy is not going to make my life miserable for three months." He's funny – we got each other's jokes – he's charming, he was smart, he could be a little bit devilish and kind of get away with it. So he had all the things I felt the character needed. As far as chemistry goes it's like when a wave comes along and you catch the wave and you ride the wave. When that happens the acting process becomes really fun, but if you don't catch that wave then it's work.'

Pfeiffer plainly found *One Fine Day* to be more fun than work. There is a definite on-screen chemistry between them. It may have helped that he knew her slightly from having dated her sister several years earlier. But whatever chemistry existed between them was confined solely to the moments when the camera was turning. There was speculation in some quarters of an on-set relationship between Clooney and Pfeiffer; one New York gossip columnist had them meeting up after hours for romantic dinners. At the time when she was supposed to be having candlelit dinners with Clooney, Pfeiffer had flown back to be with her husband – *Chicago Hope* creator David E. Kelley – and their two children.

'I loved working with George,' says Pfeiffer. 'He was charming and funny and he humanised the character, but we never even had lunch together. He'd go off to play sports with his pals and I would go and be a mom.'

Romantic rumour aside, there was plenty of other incident on the set of *One Fine Day*. The logistical problems of shooting on 44 different Manhattan locations were a nightmare without any added complications. They could have done without the pesticide which was sprayed on the grass when they were shooting in Central Park, which brought on Clooney's allergies. The allergic reaction left the actor gasping for breath and having to take refuge in a First Aid tent. They could also have done without the constant bomb threats when they decided to shoot during the Israeli Day parade; and they could certainly have done without the angry residents of New York's Upper West Side. They'd had about as much film making as they could take with Barbra Streisand's *The Mirror Has Two Faces* having just shot there as well. They took out their frustration on the *One Fine Day* crew by calling in fire alarms so that the sirens would ruin the filming.

But the one thing they could certainly have done without was the injury which almost blinded George Clooney. It came during those lunch hours which he didn't spend with Michelle Pfeiffer. Instead the sports crazy actor would go off for a pick-up game of basketball with Michael Hoffman and a few other crew members. Clooney played hard and so did everyone else. Unfortunately a crew member who was just as committed as Clooney ended up putting his elbow in the actor's eye, rupturing his eye socket and turning his left profile into a pulpy mess.

'Luckily I had six days off before going back on to the movie,' recalls Clooney. 'My eye was swollen shut and I still had to put make up on it for a long time to cover the purple bruising. I was still shooting *ER* at the time and I had to do things like hold a baby in front of my eye until the swelling went down.'

The basketball incident left Clooney with a slight but noticeable disability. Sharp-eyed *ER* fans may notice that towards the end of series two and in some early scenes in series three Clooney has a left eye which tracks slightly slower than the right. The problem has now corrected itself but Clooney was fortunate not to have sustained any more serious injury and the movie was lucky not to have lost any time because of his injury. It would not be the first time, however, that Clooney's enthusiasm for sports would give his director anxious moments through injury.

It goes without saying that by this stage George Clooney was Hollywood's most eligible bachelor. He was being voted sexiest man alive and picking up other similar titles in almost every woman's magazine. There was an intense fascination about his personal life and the tabloids and the gossip columnists were eager to seize on anything true or not – like the alleged relationship with Pfeiffer – and run with it. No one missed the irony of America's seemingly most confirmed bachelor once again surrounding himself with children who require his care.

Clooney spends a large part of his working life on television with children and here he was again in *One Fine Day* sharing almost all of his scenes with Alex Linz and Mae Whitman. 'It can be awfully hard,' says Clooney candidly of working with kids. 'It's not even about whether they're any good because most of the time kids can be good, because they can be very honest. It's just getting them to concentrate or pay attention. These kids are pros,' says Clooney of Whitman and Linz. 'There's also a fine line between kids who are pros and kids who come off like pros. I think there is something very obnoxious about the little professional kid actor. I think both of these kids come off very likeable and real. Mae Whitman is the most remarkable actress you will ever see,' he says with genuine admiration. 'She's not just an amazing kid actress, she is an amazing actress. She can do it all. Michael Hoffman would say "Cry for us" and she'd say "Okay, hang on", then she'll cry. And he'll say "Give me thirty per cent less," so she says "Okay," and she'll do thirty per cent less. I hate her,' says Clooney in mock frustration.

Clooney, however, did look after Whitman as if she was his own daughter on the set. Her big crying scene wasn't quite as simple as he suggests. While Whitman worked herself up into the proper emotional state Clooney got down on the floor with her to shield her from the potentially intimidating stare of the camera lens. Only when she was ready did he get out of the way and give Hoffman a signal that she was okay.

There were times on the set of *One Fine Day* when as many as 20 babies plus their nannies would turn up at the same time. Clooney, who swears he will never have children, says the host of infants did not stir any long dormant paternal feelings. 'It had just the opposite effect,' he laughs. 'It made me think "Thank God I don't have kids." I'm a fun uncle,' he insists. 'I get all the fun because they only see me once in a while. Then I come into the trailer, sit down, and their parents have to take them home and discipline them and do all the things I don't want to be responsible for. I just think kids are the ultimate responsibility,' says Clooney of his 'no kids' pledge. 'I think unless it's something that you absolutely have burning in you to do, you shouldn't just do it in a half-assed kind of way. I don't really feel like messing up someone's life, you know.'

Clooney is doubtless sincere in his protestations but there are those who know him who simply don't believe him. There's his father for one. He believes that Clooney will one day be swept off his feet by the right girl and once that happens then a family will follow.

Michelle Pfeiffer also sees Clooney as a future father and she is prepared to put her money where her mouth is. 'I bet George Clooney $10,000 that he is going to have children by the time he is forty,' she says. 'I wasn't kidding him. I know he will have children. There's a saying about protesting too loud. He just talks about it too much for it to be real, you know what I mean? He's going to have a gazillion kids,' she says firmly. 'I know it. And he'll be a good father. That whole thing of "I don't want to have kids" is all for show.'

Chapter 26:
A Close Call

It is to the credit of everyone concerned with *ER*, and not just George Clooney, that the show continued to go from strength to strength in its second series. A number of strong storylines, including Doug Ross's dramatic rescue of the drowning child and his subsequent relationship with his father, meant the ratings continued to rise as the show gained in popularity.

By the end of the second series, *ER* was officially America's number one television show. It had overtaken *Seinfeld* which had been the previous year's number one show. It had also set a television trend by becoming short-hand for an accepted television format. Shows could now be pitched quite legitimately as '*ER* in a squad room' or '*ER* in a fire station'. Indeed one of Steven Spielberg's subsequent and less successful series *High Incident* might reasonably be described as '*ER* with patrol cars'.

The quality of the second series was again reflected in that year's Emmy awards, with *ER* finally being recognised as Best Drama – the award Clooney felt it should have won in its debut season. But this time round, there were no awards for any of the cast, which would doubtless have rankled Clooney again. Not for himself but he felt strongly that Anthony Edwards in particular should get some kind of recognition for the work he had been doing for two years now.

The popularity of the show meant that Clooney and the others became inextricably linked in the minds of the public with the characters they played. Clooney was so popular, and fans felt they knew him so well, that on one occasion a complete stranger came up to him and asked him to be best man at his wedding. Occasionally, though, there was a slightly more hazardous side to it when fans expected them to act like doctors in medical emergencies.

On one occasion the blurring between real life and fantasy almost ended in tragedy for Anthony Edwards' three-year-old son, Bailey. Edwards and Clooney were lunching together in a Chicago restaurant during a break from shooting and Edwards' son was with them. While Clooney went to make a phone call, little Bailey got a potato crisp stuck in his throat. The child started to choke, Edwards started to panic, but other diners did nothing because they thought they were real doctors. When Clooney came back from his phone call he realised what was happening. He remembered his mother dealing with a similar childhood emergency and he turned the choking toddler upside down and thumped his back to dislodge the offending crisp.

'I thank God for George,' said Edwards later. 'Without his quick thinking I'm not sure what I would have done. Bailey was turning blue and I just panicked. I jumped up and looked for help but another diner shouted "You're a doctor. Do something!" But, despite all those lives my character saves every week, I had no idea what to do. I owe George everything,' said a grateful Edwards.

A lot of doctors, especially surgeons, develop what is known as a 'God complex'. Their constant familiarity with making life or death decisions, and the power that they wield when they have a scalpel in their hands and a patient's life at their mercy, can lead to a skewed and not entirely healthy view of reality. Actors working on a medical drama can develop similar symptoms according to Clooney.

'I don't think playing a doctor has generated any interest in medicine on my part,' he says. 'But you do start to think you can cure anything because, whenever we're in a trauma scene, all the "atmosphere people" around us are all real doctors. We go in in the morning and we learn two or three trauma scenes. We learn all of the procedures we have to do; intubating, chest compression. And you find out exactly, for example, that your hands have to be sterile at such and such a point.

'You literally are getting a medical lesson every day,' he continues. 'There are certain things that I could definitely do. No doubt about it. Actually it's a little harder for us on the show because you can't really do that stuff to an extra laying on a gurney in the studio. You can't really do a chest compression; you have to fake it. So there is a little more David Copperfield in what we do than in what happens in real life. But my friends come over and they say things like "I don't feel so good" and I just say

"Yeah, right",' Clooney complains mildly.

Clooney had very little time to bask in the success of the second series of *ER*. When everyone else had finished shooting he was still working on *One Fine Day*. Then almost immediately after wrapping the romantic comedy with Michelle Pfeiffer he found himself in *The Peacemaker*. 'I finished *One Fine Day* on May 17 and on May 21 I started work on *The Peacemaker*,' says Clooney, obviously thankful that he is a quick study and not given to Method-style absorption in the roles he plays. 'So,' he adds ironically, 'I really had a lot of time to get in shape.'

Clooney actually didn't need that much time to work out or pump up. His rigorous work schedule since the beginning of March and his constant games of basketball meant there was scarcely an ounce of fat on him. Which was no bad thing because *The Peacemaker* was one of the most physical roles he had taken to date.

The film is a post-Cold war drama based on an unpublished story from *Vanity Fair* magazine. There was a lot riding on this film, not the least of which was the fact that it marked DreamWorks' high profile entry into film production. Spielberg, Katzenberg and Geffen had been talking for months, now it was time to put up or shut up.

The Peacemaker was a prestige production from start to finish. It was being produced by Branko Lustig, who had co-produced *Schindler's List*. The script was written by Michael Schiffer, who had just had a huge hit with *Crimson Tide*, Clooney's co-star was Nicole Kidman, and the director was someone who Clooney knew well, Mimi Leder. She was one of the regular pool of *ER* directors and along with Rod Holcomb she was probably the pick of the bunch. She had won an Emmy for her handling of the classic *Love's Labors Lost* episode and was making her feature debut with *The Peacemaker*. On top of all this, *The Peacemaker* was the film that Steven Spielberg had gone to bat for at Universal to get Clooney out of a signed contract to do *The Green Hornet*.

According to the journalists who wrote the original article – Leslie and Andrew Cockburn – this nuclear blackmail story is based on actual events which had recently been disclosed in various government documents and official news sources.

George Clooney plays Colonel Thomas Devoe, a member of the American Army's crack Special Forces unit. Nicole Kidman is Dr Julia Kelly, a nuclear physicist and acting head of the top secret White House Nuclear Smuggling Group (NSG). A train carrying Russian nuclear missiles to be dismantled and scrapped is destroyed by an unexplained nuclear explosion in an isolated part of Southern Russia. The explosion triggers an alert in Washington and the NSG is put on standby. Faced with the unthinkable consequence that one of the weapons may be in the hands of a terrorist, Kelly and Devoe – who naturally enough don't see eye to eye initially – team up to track down the weapon before the terrorists can send an unmistakable threat by blowing up the United Nations building in New York.

Second-unit filming on *The Peacemaker* had begun in Eastern Europe in April but principal photography didn't begin until May when Clooney and Kidman reported for duty. Kidman wasn't initially keen to do the movie but the fact that Clooney was to be her co-star helped tip the scales. 'It's his eyes,' says Kidman. 'He can say so much without actually saying a word. You can't stop looking at him.'

Shooting *The Peacemaker* took Clooney and Kidman all over Europe, spending a lot of time in Slovakia as well as the war-torn remnants of the former Yugoslavia. The film shot in Macedonia and Croatia and one of the few bright spots during the shoot in those tragic countries came when both Clooney and Kidman managed to swing a 48-hour pass. They flew to London to celebrate the European premiere of *Mission : Impossible*, starring and produced by Kidman's husband, Tom Cruise. The three of them marked the Fourth of July in a very untypical fashion with a lavish party in that most British of establishments, Harrods department store. For the Cruises, it was a chance to relax for a few hours, but Clooney found himself the centre of attention. He also found himself linked romantically but spuriously with British television presenter and minor celebrity Dani Behr. After partying the night away at Harrods, Clooney, Kidman and Cruise flew out the following morning and it was back to front-line duty in Macedonia.

'Tom Cruise was there the whole time,' says Clooney of *The Peacemaker* shoot. 'Tom and I played a lot of basketball. I think Tom was bored but Nicole would always say "You boys go have fun," so we would play ball. Nicole is great, she's a lot of fun but she is also the consummate professional.'

DreamWorks had a lot riding on *The Peacemaker*, especially two high-priced stars who were too valuable to risk under any circumstances. Clooney had done a lot of his own stunt work in *From Dusk Till Dawn* and had wanted to do his own stunts, as much as he was able at least, on *The Peacemaker*. A horrified Steven Spielberg quickly ruled out that idea, much to the gratitude of Warner Brothers' television heads who were as anxious as Spielberg that Clooney make it through unscathed.

The wisdom of Spielberg's decision seems self-evident, but if any proof were needed it came on the day when the stunt people doubling for both Clooney and Kidman were both injured in the same stunt. The scene called for Clooney's Colonel Devoe and Kidman's Dr Kelly to jump through the stained-glass window of a church only seconds before it explodes behind them. The two stunt doubles made it through the window but appeared not to get sufficiently far away from the building before it blew. Both of them were injured when they were cut by flying glass.

Kidman and Clooney who had been watching the scene were horrified. In the siege mentality of a long shoot, much of it on location, both stars had become very friendly with the men and women who would be taking their risks for them. Kidman, as one of the few women on the set, had become especially friendly with her double and rushed to comfort her as she wandered around dazed and with blood streaming from a number of cuts. The actress burst into tears with the shock of the accident. Clooney was also said to be visibly shocked and badly shaken by what had happened.

Something had gone wrong or been misjudged or mistimed, but the professionalism of the two stunt people was enough to make sure they could ride the fall and keep their injuries to a minimum. It's hard to say what might have happened had the same stunt been done by Clooney who, although enthusiastic, doesn't have the innate sense of self-preservation of a professional stunt man. It's reasonable to assume that it would have required an enormous slice of luck for Clooney to have come off so lightly.

After the accident, in which, thankfully, neither of the doubles was seriously hurt, Clooney was heard to remark that he now understood why this sort of work was best left to the experts. The stunt people themselves were able to go back to work after some treatment for cuts and bruises.

The rest of filming on *The Peacemaker* passed without incident and the film was safely into post-production and due for a release towards the end of 1997. Clooney for his part was starting to feel the strain. With *ER*, *One Fine Day* and now *The Peacemaker*, he had been working solidly for almost nine months. For five months – from March to July – he had been working seven days a week most weeks trying to juggle his film and television commitments. He needed a break and he was just about to snatch a few days R & R.

Before that, though, there was to be another rumour about his love life. Clooney found himself linked in the supermarket tabloids with supermodel turned actress Elle Macpherson. The leggy Australian had fallen for Clooney, it was alleged, when he dropped into the Fashion Café in New York which is part owned by Macpherson. She, it is also claimed, had just been dumped by Kevin Costner and immediately set her cap at Clooney.

According to the tabloids they started dating and spent what were coyly described as 'nights of bliss' at Casa de Clooney. It was also claimed that he had wangled her a part in *Batman and Robin* because he couldn't bear to be parted from her. However, she then, apparently, found him in bed with another blonde but, instead of reading the riot act, Macpherson supposedly decided to win him back by making him jealous. She then, so the tabloids said, flaunted herself with a wealthy Swiss businessman in the hope that Clooney would come to his senses.

It was a tabloid dream. Unfortunately, says Clooney, none of it is true. Not quite none of it. He had met Macpherson once, in a bar. The second time they met was on her first day on the set of *Batman and Robin*, in which he had absolutely no say in the casting.

'So little of this stuff is true,' says Clooney with genuine sadness. 'I wish I had gotten to go to bed with Elle Macpherson and all the women they've had me going to bed with. That would have been good fun. Dammit,' he adds in mock frustration. 'What a rip off.'

It would not be long however before Clooney was once again linked with a young woman in the tabloids. This time it would be true and this time the always obliging, media-friendly Clooney would decide that his patience was running out and enough was enough.

Chapter 27:
A Paris Match

George Clooney has never wanted for company. Growing up he was the cutest child on the block and he was used to being the centre of attention either at home or at whatever broadcasting organisation his father was working for at the time.

When he went to high school it was no different. The girls used to queue up to walk him or just even to watch him walk home. He has carried that attraction through into adult life: Clooney's good looks, attentiveness and easy charm mean that women tend naturally to gravitate towards him. That ability to talk to women and to make them feel at ease in his company has led to a tabloid reputation as a womaniser which is largely unjustified.

The high-profile women with whom he has been romantically involved include Kelly Preston, Talia Balsam, DeDee Pfeiffer, Denise Crosby and Kimberly Russell. Those with whom he has been fictitiously linked make a much more interesting selection. They read like a who's who of glamorous Hollywood. There are supermodels like Elle Macpherson, Naomi Campbell and Vendela, there are actresses like Julianne Phillips, Courtney Cox, Lisa Kudrow, Michelle Pfeiffer and Nicollette Sheridan, and there are celebrities like Karen Duffy of MTV.

But far and away the most bizarre linkage between Clooney and an eligible woman came when it was suggested that he had become the latest love object of the Duchess of York. Sarah Ferguson, while she was in Los Angeles promoting her autobiography, was allegedly smitten with Clooney. It happened when they were both in the Four Seasons Hotel in Beverly Hills. Clooney was doing press for *One Fine Day* while the Duchess was promoting the book. Ferguson was taken with Clooney and according to one tabloid arranged a meeting while they were both in the hotel.

It's difficult to gauge how much credence should be given to this kind of story. It appears to be a thinly constructed fiction built upon two facts and an ill-judged remark from Clooney. The first fact is that they were both in the same hotel at roughly the same time. The second fact is that, when she was interviewed on *The Tonight Show* by Jay Leno, the newly-divorced Duchess was asked who she would most like to date now that she was single. Without a moment's hesitation she replied George Clooney. Later, when Clooney was asked about the Duchess's interest he said 'She wants to sleep with me.'

Clooney likes to joke and this appears to have been a flip answer to a question he felt wasn't worth answering but to which he did not wish to appear rude by treating with the contempt it deserved. However, surely with his experience, and with the profile he now had he should have realised that there are some things that you don't joke about. There are so many things which Clooney has said in jest and which have come back to bite him after being reported literally by an American media bereft of irony. You might think he would have got the point by now. As for Sarah Ferguson's claim that she wanted to date George Clooney, she would not be alone. She was only giving voice to a fantasy shared by a large percentage of the female population.

It's not just the female population which is attracted to George Clooney either. Since he burst onto the international scene in *ER* he has become a gay icon; a situation which is not likely to be improved by his appearance in *Batman and Robin* clad from head to foot in form-fitting rubber. This is something he has become used to. It started when he was a good-looking teenager back in Augusta.

He told *GQ* magazine that he first noticed it when he was standing backstage at Beef and Boards, the dinner theatre at which his father would occasionally perform. 'I was this 15-year-old kid,' he explained, 'and there were all these chorus boys from *Fiddler on the Roof* being really nice to me. Then,' he added, 'I realised what was going on.'

The same-sex come-on and his attractiveness to gay men would follow him through his career. His mailbag on *ER* is generously weighted towards eager female admirers but he also has a significant amount of fan mail from gay men. There is, according to *Entertainment Weekly* magazine, a letter framed and hanging in the upstairs hallway of his house. 'Dear George Clooney,' it reads. 'You are my favourite star. I love you. I love homosexual men. I love homosexual actors.' The letter then apparently goes on to list, in unstinting detail, just exactly what the writer would love to see Clooney doing on the show.

There is not a single scrap of evidence to suggest even remotely that George Clooney is anything other than seriously heterosexual. He appears now – after one bad marriage and a damaging lengthy relationship – to be a confirmed bachelor in the literal sense of the expression. He has the good fortune, or misfortune depending on which side of the fence you are standing, to have the sort of appeal onto which every one – straight female or gay male – can project their own private sexual fantasies. It is a cross he does not bear alone. It is the sort of accusation which is also levelled, without substantiation, at other Nineties heartthrobs like Keanu Reeves and Richard Gere. Sadly for them, all the denials in the world would do no good at all. They simply have to get on with their lives.

Clooney, though, is a little tired of hearing his name linked with every female with a pulse within a hundred yards of him. 'Every single week I'm on the cover of *National Enquirer* with some girl,' he says with only slight exaggeration, 'and a lot of times we've never even met before. It's all "He grabbed her and she turned around and smiled and he said 'You're wearing plaid'." It's all so specific.

'And the problem is,' he continues, 'it's very hard for me to sit there and say to someone I'm dating "It didn't happen." Because I always grew up reading those things myself thinking "There is probably some element of truth in that."'

Clooney of course had already been potentially damaged before when his alleged racist remarks to an extra on the set of *ER* were blown up in the tabloids. 'The girl that I was going out with at the time was black, but that isn't a defence,' says Clooney, trying to articulate the dilemma facing high profile media targets. 'You can't say "Oh, I'm dating a black person", because that doesn't prove anything. The defence is that it never happened. Eventually they printed a retraction because it didn't happen. But I am now burned because of that,' he says.

There was one recurring story in the tabloids in the summer of 1996 which linked Clooney romantically with a new woman in his life. This time it turned out to be true. French beauty Céline Balitran made her debut in the American tabloids when Clooney took her to an awards ceremony as his date. They had met when Clooney was in Paris snatching a quick break between shooting *The Peacemaker* and *Batman and Robin*. Clooney was fairly unequivocal about how he spent his time. 'I would go into a café and drink until it closed,' he said. 'Then I would sit in another one and drink coffee until I sobered up.'

But in the course of his sojourn in the city of love, Clooney found love himself. The 23-year-old blonde Balitran was working part-time at Barfly, a trendy Parisian diner, when Clooney walked in. 'As soon as I saw him I cracked,' Balitran told *Paris Match* magazine. 'He smiled at me and I smiled at him. We looked at each other and couldn't take our eyes away.'

Clooney, who had once claimed that he had never formally asked a woman out and that all of his dates had been with people he knew, apparently came back every day for a week before he finally got up the nerve to ask Balitran out. 'We went for a walk and suddenly he seized me in his arms and kissed me,' says Balitran, who appears to have found Clooney in Doug Ross mode momentarily. 'At that precise moment,' she continued, 'I realised he was the man of my life.'

There was some confusion about Clooney's new love when the story was reported in America. The tabloids in particular couldn't seem to make up their minds about what she did for a living. Some said she was a barmaid, others said she was a lawyer, while there were some who said she was a nursery teacher. The truth is that she was a former nursery teacher who was now studying law and had been working in Barfly during her holidays.

George Clooney was once quoted to the effect that he didn't quite understand his own sex appeal. 'I'm still amazed by all the fuss,' he said. 'I can't remember the last time I went out on a normal date with a girl. Every single day I am linked with all these beautiful women. But the truth is that it's very hard to find love in Hollywood.'

All of that was said pre-Céline. Clooney, who found it hard to find love in LA, had obviously decided to broaden his search and moved his hunt to Europe where he struck it lucky. He and Balitran were instantly attracted and before too long she had packed her bags and moved to Los Angeles to be closer to him.

Coming from Paris to Los Angeles must have been something of a culture shock to Balitran. Discovering that your new boyfriend is the toast of Hollywood must have been an even bigger surprise. Clooney tried, as far as he was able, to protect her from the intrusion of the paparazzi. When they were out in public at a formal occasion then they both accepted they were fair game for the snappers, but in private it was a different matter. 'I have actually said to her "Hang in there,"' says Clooney. 'Dating me is a hassle.'

So much of a hassle, apparently, that whenever she goes to visit him she takes a convoluted route and then drives past his house. Only when she is sure she isn't being followed will she then double back and go in. On other occasions Clooney has found photographers attempting to climb over his perimeter fence to get pictures of the two of them together.

Céline Balitran appears to be made of stern stuff and gives the impression of being around for the long haul. But even just by being George Clooney's girlfriend she has become a news story in herself by the standards of tabloid journalism. 'It doesn't stop,' says Clooney. 'Céline even gets stories about her in the Paris newspapers saying things like she's kicked the pig out, and kicked out all my friends. For I while I think the tabloids bothered her,' says Clooney sympathetically, 'but she is such a trouper and she is handling it really well.'

The one bone of contention, according to the tabloids at least, is Max. Balitran and the pig, it's alleged, don't get on and she has apparently given Clooney an ultimatum on more than one occasion to choose between her and the pig. Clooney, who jokingly says it would be a tough choice, says this is simply not true. To be fair to him he's had Max for ten years, that's longer than any of his girlfriends have stuck it out.

After Clooney and Balitran had been together for about six months the tabloids decided it was time they got married. Clooney, they said, had fallen head over heels in love and was ready to propose, possibly before the end of the year.

It would appear that Céline had certainly been thinking along those lines. In that *Paris Match* story she said that she and Clooney had realised they could not live without each other. 'We are madly in love,' she was reported as saying, 'and for me a love story means marriage and babies.'

But while she was being quoted as saying that in *Paris Match*, Clooney was sticking to the party line in Los Angeles. 'It's not for me,' he said of marriage, 'I was married once and I wasn't very good at it. I have a great girlfriend now. We get along well. Why mess with that? For me the bottom line is, children are great. I'm a good uncle, I love kids, but I believe if you're going to be a parent there has to be something in you that says "I have to have children."'

Clooney obviously believes – even if others like Michelle Pfeiffer don't – that whatever that genetic imperative is, then it is missing in him. But while he was promoting *One Fine Day* one journalist came out and asked him flatly about any wedding plans. 'The wedding?' said Clooney. 'We'll hold off on that thanks. The pig has to die first and they live for thirty years.'

Chapter 28:
Tabloid Wars

George Clooney is apparently fond of saying that 'he gets the joke' these days. By that he's suggesting that he knows the score, he knows he is flavour of the month, he knows that at the moment the sun is shining and he is determined to make hay.

There must be times, however, when he wishes that other people – especially the American press – got the joke too. Clooney likes to joke. He always has. But it seems like every time he has said something in jest – like Sarah Ferguson wanting to sleep with him – it becomes slavishly reported as the gospel truth. He once, for example, described his movie debut *And They're Off!* as 'a film about geldings'. A schoolboy pun but it was reported as fact. It was the same with George Clooney's vasectomy – or non-vasectomy as the case may be.

Michelle Pfeiffer had bet Clooney $10,000 that he would have children by the time he was 40. When Nicole Kidman heard about this on the set of *The Peacemaker* she decided this was too good to pass up. She wanted a piece of the action too so she put up $10,000 of her money for a similar bet. The matter was raised with Clooney when he was doing press for *One Fine Day*. Clooney's reply was entirely in jest. 'No way am I going to lose any money on this one,' he told a reporter. 'I figure, here's the deal, I get a vasectomy for five grand and I'm $15,000 up right there and then.'

It was a joke. But almost before the words were out of his mouth the 'George Clooney to get snip' stories were winging their way round the world's tabloids. Clooney is not alone in being taken literally. Nick Nolte once famously and patiently wound up a reporter from a high-toned magazine about a new cosmetic surgery procedure he had just undergone. Sure enough the magazine article appeared with a detailed and sympathetic account of the star's non-existent testicle tuck. You can argue that Nolte was being malicious but Clooney was simply trying to brighten up everyone's day in the unremitting ordeal of a press junket.

He could be forgiven if perhaps his patience was starting to wear thin. He continued to play his part in the great game of hype by which movie stars live or die but it was becoming more difficult. The media were becoming more and more intrusive about his relationship with Céline Balitran and once *Batman and Robin* started shooting at the beginning of September 1996, the pressure became almost unbearable. Eventually Clooney decided he had had enough.

On October 24, Clooney wrote a letter to Linda Bell Blue, the executive producer of *Entertainment Tonight*, the world's most successful syndicated entertainment news and gossip show. The letter caused a bombshell in Hollywood. The text of the letter was leaked to *Entertainment Weekly* magazine and it is worth quoting in full:

Well, we gave it a shot. And for a six month period Frank Kelly kept his word. My name wasn't on *Hard Copy* and I did several interviews for you. I guess the statute of limitations for keeping your word is about six months for Mr Kelly, or maybe it was a landmark and I should feel honoured.

Last month *Hard Copy* did an undercover story about my girlfriend and me. A probing in-depth report that will have great significance in the world. The story doesn't matter. The point is that he broke our deal. A deal that he proposed.

What is most amazing to me is that he offered this deal in the first place. In a letter! He actually wrote it down . . . A so-called news format show will agree that they will not be covering me in future stories, if I do his *other* show.

Now that's amazing!

If you're going to call a show *Hard Copy*, implying some sort of journalistic and ethical investigating, you can't make deals to certain people not to put them on your show . . . or at least you can't write it down. What an idiot.

So now we begin. Officially. No interviews from this date on. Nothing on *ER*, nothing from *One Fine Day*, nothing from *Batman and Robin*, and nothing from Dreamworks' (sic) first film, *The Peacemaker*. These interviews will be reserved for all press but you. *Access Hollywood*,

E!, whoever. It won't affect you much. Maybe other actors will join me. Maybe not. That doesn't matter, it's about doing what's right.

Again, I am sorry. You're a nice bunch of people and you have always treated me fairly. But your company and Mr Kelly have to be responsible for what they say and who they say it to.

And so do I.

Clooney's letter caused a sensation and made headlines around the world. Here was an actor having the temerity to stand up to a television show, someone willing to deprive himself of the oxygen of publicity to make a point.

But it was not a spur of the moment reaction. There was a history between the actor and some of the producers at Paramount's television division, which makes both *Entertainment Tonight* and *Hard Copy*. As he says in the letter, George Clooney's complaint wasn't really with *Entertainment Tonight*, which is not known for its savage or incisive reporting of the entertainment scene. He was, however, upset with *Hard Copy*, the market leader in America's booming tabloid television industry. And this was not the first time he had made the threat. As early as February 1996, Clooney had written to Linda Bell Blue complaining that he was appearing on *Hard Copy* about once a week. As he pointed out to Bell Blue at the time, there was little he could do to limit *Hard Copy* – constitutionally they are allowed to report what they like – but he could deny the sister show, *Entertainment Tonight*, any access.

Paramount, which produces both shows, wrote back within a fortnight. The letter from *Hard Copy* producer Frank Kelly says, according to *USA Today* newspaper, 'We agree that *Hard Copy* will not be covering you on any future stories.'

However on September 23 *Hard Copy* ran footage of Clooney and Balitran on the set of *Batman and Robin*. The footage had been gathered by a new breed of celebrity pests – the 'stalkerazzi' or 'videorazzis'. A number of Hollywood stars including Robert De Niro, Cher, Alec Baldwin and Madonna had been hounded by these video stalkers. Their aim is to provoke stars to violence and then catch the assault on video and sell it to a tabloid show like *Hard Copy*. Since he made the big time, and certainly since he took up with Balitran, Clooney had been a stalkerazzi staple.

'People yell out horrible things,' he explained to *USA Today*. 'I'm able to take it when they say "Hey George are you a homosexual?" I just smile and keep walking because I don't want them to make money off of me. But when I'm with my secretary and they yell "Does she give good head?" Then suddenly – I grew up in Kentucky and there's a guy in me that goes "You have to defend that person." I think the video paparazzi cross a line a lot now. 'I live a good life, and I'm lucky and I expect some times to be difficult,' said Clooney in another interview. 'I know that people will jump out and take pictures of you – I've seen that with my family. What is different now are these video paparazzi. These young kids with video cameras are not journalists. I'll be walking with my girlfriend and they'll say "Who's the fat chick?" They want me to walk over to them so they can have a confrontation and sell the footage.'

Although not quite in the category of Emile Zola's 'J'accuse' letter, Clooney's missive had brought into the open an uncomfortable and unpleasant fact of Hollywood life. Only the week before he wrote his letter the stalkerazzi had staked out the house next door to Madonna to get pictures of her and her new baby and the tape duly appeared on *Hard Copy*. Madonna acknowledged in a statement that there was a price to pay for being in the public eye, but she felt that a line had been crossed.

There were others who felt the same way too and Clooney, without expecting to, found himself riding the crest of a wave of support. Madonna sent a letter to *Entertainment Tonight* saying she too would refuse to do interviews, as did Whoopi Goldberg. Clooney's friend Dean Cain, who plays *Superman* on television, offered his support, as did Steven Spielberg. In a statement Spielberg said he was joining Clooney's boycott because 'It beats litigation. For too long,' said Spielberg, 'garbage has been on sale at outrageous prices.'

Warner Brothers, the studio making *Batman and Robin*, also played their part by calling in the police to arrest three people it claimed were secretly taking pictures on the set. Two men had been arrested after allegedly taping Arnold Schwarzenegger, who was playing the villainous Mr Freeze. A woman was also taken into custody after studio security guards allegedly found her with a tape of Clooney. The arrests came only days after a behind-the-scenes video featuring the two actors had appeared on another tabloid television show, *Inside Edition*. The three were all expected to face criminal charges.

The freedom of the American press is enshrined in the First Amendment of the Constitution. Clooney was certainly not trying to interfere with that. What he was trying to do was to get *Hard Copy* and other shows like it to stop buying stalkerazzi footage. 'When you take away the demand, the supply slows down,' he said.

Clooney's actions may have been motivated by down-home decency, a sense that he should stand up for others who couldn't stand up for themselves. But in doing so he showed, as if anyone needed to know , just how influential he now was – and not just because of the friends he had. Within ten days of Clooney's letter to *Entertainment Tonight*, Paramount released a statement to the effect that *Hard Copy* would no longer pay for or air footage from videorazzis. It was a decision apparently inspired by pragmatism rather than nobility but, whatever their reasons, Clooney had won and his colleagues throughout the entertainment industry were grateful for the stand he took.

Clooney wasn't letting the matter rest there. He had had a similar deal with *Hard Copy* before, after all, and it had lasted only six months. This time round he warned the producers of the show that he would be keeping an eye on them to make sure they kept their promise.

'Every single night I tape them and watch them,' he said six weeks later. 'They're completely different now, and seem to have honoured the thing they said they would do. And we'll see if they stick it out a little longer.'

Clooney and his people had an ongoing series of meetings with the *Hard Copy* producers after the incident to make sure that everyone was clear on what was being done. The actor claimed that his case only gave Paramount the opportunity to do a little bit of house-cleaning they had wanted to do for some time without ever having an excuse.

'It sounds very petty,' Clooney concedes, 'because no one really wants to hear from someone who things are going well for. But I did it because I wanted people to be responsible for what they say. My father wrote for a newspaper,' Clooney pointed out, 'and still has a column three days a week in the *Cincinnati Post*. It's my favourite profession. I think it's better than government – I think it's more important. And I watch it getting the lines crossed now. All I'm saying is that people should be responsible for what they say,' Clooney continues. 'If *Inside Edition* themselves had broken into the Bat-set, and stolen badges, and passes, and walkie talkies, and footage and then run it, they would have been held responsible for what they did. Instead the three 17-year-old kids who did it will go to jail. And *Inside Edition* will use the footage. I don't believe in censorship,' says Clooney forcefully, 'and I don't believe in telling people that they can't do something. I hate that idea and I don't ever want to be allowed that right. I was just not going to help *Entertainment Tonight* make money to use that money to buy footage of me. That isn't fair.'

Clooney also revealed while he was promoting *One Fine Day* that he always believed *Hard Copy* would renege on their original agreement which is why he held on to the letter from Frank Kelly. He also picked his moment in terms of when he would play his trump card.

'It was an innocuous story, it meant nothing, didn't hurt me at all,' says Clooney of the footage of himself and Balitran which appeared on *Hard Copy* and prompted his letter to *Entertainment Tonight*. 'That was important, because I didn't want it to be about me sleeping with the pig. I didn't want it to be about some stupid story, I wanted it to be about the issues.

'I sent back the second letter and a lot of journalists picked up on it, I think because I wasn't talking about censorship,' says Clooney. 'I wasn't hitting anybody. I wasn't taking a shotgun and pointing it at anyone. I was just saying "Now I have some evidence here and this evidence says that these people who call themselves journalists are not. They are entertainers." And that's fine,' he adds. 'If that's what you want to call yourself, then call yourself *Entertainment Tonight* and do a show like that. Call yourself *The Gossip Show* on E! But don't call yourself news.'

There was one other brush with the tabloids while *Batman and Robin* was shooting, but this time it was with a newspaper. A young woman called Kim Weiant sold her story to the tabloids, claiming to have been a former Clooney girlfriend. The point of her story was that she and Clooney had gone to bed on several occasions but they never actually had sex. 'George would never love me like a real man,' she complained. The truth of the matter appears to be that the unfortunate woman was an over-enthusiastic fan with an overactive imagination. It's doubtful whether she and Clooney actually met far less went to bed together. Weiant was eventually led off the *Batman* set and was expected to face trespass charges.

Clooney had started out trying to make a point about television tabloids and ended up becoming an unlikely crusader for the world's most conspicuously wealthy oppressed minority. The way people rallied to his cause came as a little bit of a shock, but a pleasant one nonetheless.

'I was surprised at how many people came on board,' said Clooney once the fuss had died down somewhat. 'I was thrilled by it and thrilled by the changes that have come along. But,' he cautioned, 'I am still very wary.'

Chapter 29:
The Caped
Crusader

*I*n a recent interview Michelle Pfeiffer was asked if she had felt it necessary to give George Clooney any advice on *One Fine Day* since it was his first time out as a leading man. She, quite properly, said that Clooney didn't need any help and besides, she pointed out, they considered themselves lucky to get him to play the lead.

However, there was one area of expertise in which she could advise him. Clooney was about to star in *Batman and Robin* and she had been over that particular ground before when she played Catwoman in *Batman Returns*. 'I just told him to make sure they give him a trapdoor in that suit, that's all, so he could go to the bathroom,' she said. 'That, and to remember to have fun, because sometimes it's hard.'

Batman and Robin started shooting on September 1 as one of the most keenly anticipated movies in years. Director Joel Schumacher was shooting on a closed set which meant there were no press and no visitors. This is as much for speed and efficiency as anything else but it does lend an air of mystique and excitement to the proceedings.

Media interest in the film was intense, and not just because there was a new Batman. This film boasted the most impressive cast of the *Batman* quartet. As well as Clooney as Batman and Chris O'Donnell returning as Robin, the villains were being played by Arnold Schwarzenegger as Mr Freeze and Uma Thurman as Poison Ivy. There was a new Bat-character too with Alicia Silverstone, fresh from her success in *Clueless*, starring as Batgirl.

One of the first priorities was the Batsuit. It had been redesigned between each of the movies and again there would be refinements for Clooney. 'George did want a new suit,' says director Joel Schumacher. 'He likes to tell people he fit into Val's suit, only the codpiece had to be made much bigger.'

Clooney thought that Pfeiffer had been joking when she said he should insist on a trapdoor but he quickly found out that she wasn't. It wasn't long before he was referring to the suit – and not with his usual jokiness – as "a miserable piece of architecture".

He tried to articulate the problems he was facing in a rare interview with *Cinescape* magazine towards the end of the shoot. 'Have you ever walked around in rubber from head to toe all day long?' he asked, one assumes rhetorically. 'I think they could call this the *Batman* diet,' Clooney continued. 'That's how hot the suit is. Buckets of sweat are pouring out of you. You feel light-headed. You can't hear a thing. Plus, with that suit, it's not a great idea to consume massive quantities of liquids, if you know what I mean.'

Clooney reportedly contacted his Bat-predecessors Michael Keaton and Val Kilmer to ask if they had any tips but both told him the only thing to do was just sweat it out. 'It was bad enough trying to squeeze into the rubber suit,' says Clooney. 'But having to leap around in it and pretend you're comfortable is much worse. It seems to shrink once you've got it on and it pinches in all the wrong places. It weighs, including the cape, about 50 pounds, and it had to be buffed constantly because of the kind of rubber it is. It also rips easily. It was so hot I had to stop several times for a mop up. They made a special wedge for me to pry open the mask and let in fresh air. During breaks between scenes I sat in front of a huge fan.'

As he had done with Val Kilmer in *Batman Forever*, Joel Schumacher promised a totally different Batman in George Clooney. Kilmer was much lighter than Keaton and Clooney is shaping up to be even lighter again. 'I think we've seen enough of the Bat-brooding,' Clooney promised during shooting. 'I mean, let's think about it for a minute. Batman doesn't have such a tough life. The guy is loaded. He gets all the best girls. He has a cool car. What does Batman have to be depressed about?'

Regardless of his light-hearted approach to the character, Clooney was intelligent enough to know that this would present him with a whole new range of challenges as an actor. 'When you do a set piece in *One Fine Day* for example,' he explains, 'you rehearse a couple of weeks, you go in and you sit down and you do three-and-a-half or four pages. A fun scene. When you do *Batman* you do an eighth of a page.'

And, as Clooney points out, most of the dialogue will be looped – dubbed on later in post-production – and the accent is on the technical. 'I think your abilities as an actor are much more important in something like *Batman and Robin*, and it's much harder to do,' he continues. 'When you have a good director and good writing most actors will come off good – if you're doing a romantic comedy, a movie with dialogue. When you're doing *Batman and Robin*, and you do have a good director and good writing, but you're doing very tiny technical things with this Batsuit which – and I'm not complaining – is a miserable piece of architecture, it is harder.

'There was one night, for example, when I was shooting with these three big fans blowing tons of plastic snow into my mouth – and you have to try and clench your teeth so it doesn't go into your lungs – but it's still in there. And you can't see and you can't hear, because you've got the suit on. You're also trying to deliver lines in this state, which you'll be looping later, and you're doing all this stuff with a stunt double and everything else. All the while you can't see in front of your face. All you're praying to do is not come out looking like a dickhead,' he says. 'And that takes a lot more skill.'

One of the creative aspects of the *Batman* movies which had irked both Keaton and Kilmer was Batman's actual lack of involvement in the movies. He was frequently reduced to what amounted to a supporting role. Clooney was much more sanguine about that. He knew that he would be overshadowed by the villains – especially the larger than life Schwarzenegger – but he was prepared for it. 'That's part of the gig. That's part of the deal,' he says pragmatically. 'That's just the way it works. Batman isn't the most interesting character in the *Batman* projects. And I probably won't be the most interesting Batman. But I get to work with a great director and I get to work with great actors. I also get to be part of one of the biggest franchises in movie history. And you know what else? I get other opportunities. What *Batman* does is give you the opportunities to do anything else you want to do. Before *One Fine Day* and before *The Peacemaker*, the publicity machine for *Batman* alone was so big. It's a major, major, major film. So for me it was a great opportunity.

'I sit there looking at this stuff – it's twice as big as the last one – and I said to Joel as we were sitting on what was the largest set I had ever seen in my life, I said: "I'm intimidated by this damn thing." And he said: "So am I. I've never seen anything this large in life." So it's fun,' Clooney concludes.

The other aspect of *Batman and Robin* which worried Clooney was appearing opposite Schwarzenegger. The two men had met socially at a number of Planet Hollywood openings and other functions. They had always got on but, as any actor will tell you, working with someone and socialising with someone can be two different things. 'You worry, especially if you're a guy, about working with a giant male star,' says Clooney candidly. 'I worried about that, because you don't know. Because things can change. I walked into this situation and Arnold has been so nice, so much fun to be around. He makes the set a blast. He's amazingly professional but he also has a great time. He has been so gracious and nice to me through this whole thing that, I tell you, I cannot say enough good things about him,' says Clooney. 'I was shocked at how gracious he has been about all of this because this is a pretty awkward place for me – I'm the third Batman.'

Schwarzenegger kept the producers of *Batman and Robin* waiting a long time as he juggled other projects to allow him to do the action block-buster. He plays Mr Freeze who has a grudge against Batman because he is tricked by Poison Ivy into believing that Batman was responsible for the death of his wife. But, speaking on the set, he said he was glad he had got involved. 'I wanted the role because it's this huge machine, it's an event movie,' says Schwarzenegger. 'I saw *Independence Day* which I loved and I thought "This is a spectacle. I want to be part of something that is just enormous." It stuns me how big this is. They drape us with sheets when we walk outside from set to set so no one can film us in costume and steal our ideas. We've had people try to break in just to steal props. The whole thing is just wild.'

But, like Clooney, Schwarzenegger found the costume to be a major problem. He insisted that his was even more problematic than Clooney's because it weighed more, he had to wear another space-suit-like costume on top of his rubber suit, and as well as all that he had to carry his Freeze-ray gun which weighed about 25 pounds on its own.

Despite the irritations of the costumes and the physical arduousness of the shoot, *Batman and Robin* seemed to go ahead without any of the tantrums or bad feeling which were a hallmark of the filming of *Batman Forever*. 'Chris and George are both nice and cool,' Schumacher told *Cinescape*. 'They're old friends. They both have a sense of humour. With some people,' he said pointedly, 'it turns out that what you see is what you get.'

Clooney was equally enthusiastic about working with Schumacher and the efforts he went to in order to prevent things getting too intense in what is, after all, an action romp. 'It's the happiest set you'll ever see,' says Clooney. 'It's amazing. Joel has this microphone and he does this Shecky Greene routine for hours. "So, anyway," he'll say. "What are we doing now?" And he goes on for hours. But it's funny, and fun, and everyone laughs all the time there. The *ER* set is exactly the same.'

'I always tell George that he is the only Batman who would be able to dress his own wounds,' Schumacher jokes, adding that his split-week between *Batman* and *ER* occasionally caused some confusion. 'When someone gets hurt in this film I have seen George looking at them a little sympathetically. I have to say "George, this is not *ER*. You are not going to fix their wound."

But it was not all sweetness and light. Clooney twice injured himself during shooting with his lunchtime pick-up basketball games. On one occasion he broke his finger then, towards the end of the shoot, he twisted his ankle. The injury kept him on crutches for several days and eventually forced Schumacher to put his foot down and ban the basketball games altogether.

The basketball games were a landmark for comic book trivia buffs. Clooney and O'Donnell were often joined by Dean Cain who was filming *The New Adventures of Superman* on a nearby sound stage. So, on the basketball court at least, you had Superman going head to head against Batman and Robin. For the record, Clooney insists that the non-super-powered Batman beat the super-powered Superman every time.

During shooting Clooney pointed out that like Batman – or more correctly, like Bruce Wayne – he now gets to live in a nice house and drive nice cars. And, even if life was difficult for him at the moment, no one really wants to hear him complain. 'I live a pretty good life,' says Clooney. 'I work a lot right now. I'm on this seven-day-a-week schedule but I have no real complaints. Life's pretty good for me. 'The bad side is really only the work,' he continued. 'It's not that I don't like doing the work. It's just that right now I'm a little bit over my head. I'm working seven days a week – that's about 100 hours a week, so I'm pretty buried. Monday, Tuesday, Wednesday, Thursday, I do *ER*, and Friday, Saturday, Sunday I do *Batman*.

'And the problem with that is that because I'm only working on those days I'm in almost every scene. So there are no breaks. You're just boom, boom, boom, working. Those are just the things that they have to accept. They say "Can you do it?" and you say "Sure, I can do it." And then you get in the middle of it. There was a time when I was sitting in the Batsuit, which is miserable, and I'm sitting in this damn thing and saying to myself "I don't know if I'm going to make it. I don't know if I'll do it." But then I got over halfway and I knew I would get it done.'

Comments about being 'over his head' again brought news stories that

Clooney was about to quit *ER*. Once again he adamantly denied them. 'I'll finish my contract,' he said categorically. 'I have a five-year contract with the show and I will honour it. It's the right thing to do. Not to mention, it's really a great show and it's a great show to be on. We really have a great time. It's hard as hell doing that show, but I love it. I love going to work every day. I love Anthony Edwards. I love those people. I love Noah Wyle.'

Shooting on *Batman and Robin* finished on schedule on January 31, 1997 and Clooney was able finally to look forward to a well-earned rest after five months of seven-day weeks. He had only one thought as the filming ended and the movie went into post-production for its June release. 'This is the fifth most successful movie franchise ever and I just hope I don't screw it up,' said Clooney. 'That would be a drag.'

Chapter 30:
A Player At Last

In the week before Christmas 1996, Bill Case made the 17-mile journey from Augusta to Maysville. He was not the only one of Augusta's 1,500 inhabitants who would make that trip in that week. This was a big event. The new George Clooney movie – *One Fine Day* – was opening and Augusta isn't big enough to have its own cinema so everyone had to go to Maysville to see it.

It was a little under 20 years since George Clooney had told Bill Case to hang on to his typing papers because he was going to be a movie star one day. Now he had made good on his promise and his old teacher was in the audience to see it. 'It was a real good feeling to see him up there on the screen,' says Case. 'I could see him doing a lot of the things his character does in that movie. There's that scene where he is in a big rush but his little girl wants to stay and play with the kittens under the table, so he stops what he's doing to spend time with her. That's just the sort of thing George would do,' says Bill Case. 'He is that kind of guy. He will always take time to make time for you, no matter how busy he is.

'The other scene that stood out was the one where he picks up Michelle Pfeiffer and throws her over his shoulder so that he and the kids can splash around in the water in the park,' says Case. 'That's exactly like George. That's his sense of fun,' says Case.

Bill Case voted *One Fine Day* a big hit and so did the critics. *Variety* described the film as 'a pretty ideal baby-boomer romantic comedy' and predicted strong box office with good staying power. *Variety* critic Todd McCarthy was particularly enthusiastic in his praise for Clooney. 'Clooney,' says the review, ' in his second post-*ER* stardom feature, makes it all look easy, effortlessly conveying both the capable, tenacious, professional side of his character and the romantic softy inside. He's the rare major actor who, like Clark Gable, holds equal appeal for men and women, and here shows a light touch that offers further evidence of considerable range and ability to dominate on the big screen.'

Given the rave reviews which the film, and especially Clooney, received, the box office returns turned out to be a little disappointing. *One Fine Day* opened in fifth place in the American box office with a gross of $6.2 million. But, as *Variety* had predicted, it had legs and remained in the top ten for five weeks and finally went on to gross $42 million in the United States with good prospects for overseas territories.

The original plan was for the film to have been released on Valentine's Day, which happily would fall on a Friday in 1997, but Fox decided to move the release up to the Christmas season. Those opening weekend figures are solid if unspectacular but there are a number of reasons for *One Fine Day* under-performing. The first and most obvious is the box office powerhouse performance of Tom Cruise's sports movie *Jerry Maguire*, which steam-rolled the competition. *Jerry Maguire* remained in the top three of the American charts for seven weeks, grossing more than $100 million in the process and sucking a lot of oxygen out of the box office. One other reason, this time put forward by the magazine *Entertainment Weekly*, was that there were three romantic comedies bidding for the same audience at the same time.

This was an almost unprecedented situation. As well as Clooney and Pfeiffer in *One Fine Day*, audiences could also choose between Denzel Washington and Whitney Houston in *The Preacher's Wife* or Jeff Bridges and Barbra Streisand in *The Mirror Has Two Faces*. So the audience was split three ways. That being the case, it is encouraging for Clooney and his backers that *One Fine Day* emerged as a clear winner in this mini-box office contest and, were it released in a weekend without romantic rivals, it would doubtless have performed much better.

One other possibility for the deflated box office returns is the pairing of Clooney and Pfeiffer itself. Michelle Pfeiffer is one of America's finest actresses but she is not, in and of herself, a box office draw. Even teamed with heavyweights like Robert Redford in *Up Close and Personal* or Al Pacino in *Frankie and Johnny*, she has failed to deliver a romantic smash. Perhaps her screen persona is a little too cool and distant for audiences to warm to in a romantic setting.

Even if, in hindsight, a Valentine weekend opening might have seemed more sensible, Clooney could still be pleased with the opening of the film and the way it had been received. He would be even more pleased by his end of year gift from Warner Brothers. Clooney formed a new production company with partner Robert Lawrence and Warner immediately signed them up to a three-year deal which would give them a first look at any projects from the new company, and the opportunity to develop and produce those projects.

The new company came about as a happy Hollywood accident. Lorenzo di Bonaventura and Bill Gerber had become co-presidents of worldwide theatrical production at Warner earlier in the year. They had been looking for projects and Lawrence, whose screen credits include *Clueless, Down Periscope* and a stint as executive producer on *Die Hard with a Vengeance*, had been pitching ideas to them. At the same time George Clooney had been looking for projects that he might produce. There was an obvious synergy so the then unnamed Clooney–Lawrence company came into being.

'George has proved himself to be an astute, instinctive and intelligent judge of material, and Robert's track record as a production executive is remarkable and includes a wide range of films,' said di Bonaventura and Gerber in a statement to *Variety*.

Although the deal is for pictures that Clooney would produce rather than appear in, there was at least one project which was grabbing his interest. It's thought that Clooney was keen to star in as well as produce a property called *Becky Downtown*, an idea from writer Ardwright Chamberlain for an *Adam's Rib*-style romantic comedy set in the world of criminal law in New York City.

The production deal at Warner Brothers, as well as his own three picture deal as an actor at the same studio, and a production commitment from NBC for him to create TV projects, established George Clooney as a Hollywood player by the end of the year. He appeared for the first time on *Entertainment Weekly's* annual list of the 100 most influential people in Hollywood. He just scraped in at number 99 between authors Patricia Cornwell and R.L. Stine. But when you consider that Oscar-winner and newly-crowned action star Nicolas Cage is ranked at only 97 then Clooney's inclusion is not to be sneezed at. In all likelihood if 1997 shapes up the way it should, he can look forward to being at least several places higher in the magazine's next list.

Clooney actually appeared in a lot of year-end lists. *People* magazine listed him in their honour roll of people of the year for his stand against the talkerazzi. And countless magazines chose him as their Hunk of the Year. He also found himself voted sexiest man alive by one British women's magazine. Clooney's reaction to this sort of thing is well documented and, as he might say himself, at least he's not being voted Schmuck of the Year.

The man who once thought his dreams had passed him by would take more satisfaction from his inclusion in the *Entertainment Weekly* poll. Not for his position on it, but simply for the fact that he was on it. He was being recognised as a man of substance, a man to be taken seriously. The young man who had left Augusta against his parents' wishes with stars in his eyes had matured and changed and emerged as a responsible adult.

In *One Fine Day*, a frustrated and harassed Michelle Pfeiffer accuses Clooney – or at least accuses Jack Taylor – of having a Peter Pan complex. That's an accusation that might have been levelled at Clooney himself with some justification. The man who got married in Vegas by an Elvis impersonator and then hung out with his bachelor pals and his pet pig certainly does appear to be suffering from that kind of syndrome.

But the man who was prepared to work seven days a week for the better part of a year is no Peter Pan. The man with the hit TV series, the three-movie deal, and the production deal with two studios is a serious, committed professional. Bear in mind that while Clooney is pushing himself to do other work on top of *ER* there are others – like actress Sherry Stringfield – who have decided to leave the show because they find the schedule of doing *ER* on its own too demanding. This new George Clooney may be the influence of Céline Balitran, who apparently has him eating properly and regularly and going for long mountain bike rides. It is more likely that he is just getting older. Peter Pan is growing up.

Clooney has always joked about his fame being transient. He knows that more than anyone; he has seen it happen. He's the first to offer a quip about being back on *Hollywood Squares* or serving in a fast food joint. But it does look as though in his case now he has reached the point where he is immune to his own theory of 'And then tragedy struck'. He has learned lessons, he has seen it happen to others, and he has been fortunate that fame has come at a time when he was sufficiently mature to make the best use of it.

As his teenage girl friend Laura Laycock says, George Clooney can be thankful to be a small town boy. That Southern friendliness goes with him wherever he is,' says Laycock, 'and I think that has a lot to do with his attitude. He hasn't changed, he's still the same way. When he comes home he always stops to talk, he always asks after your children, he always wants to get together. His parents will invite different classmates up to the house for lunch when George is home and they'll just sit and talk. But they never talk about life in California,' says Laycock, 'because he just wants to talk about the old days in school, and sit around and laugh about the different things we did. He just wants to sit back, put his feet up, and be George.

'He doesn't take anything for granted and I think those are small town values,' she says. 'He grew up here and his roots are here. He knows who his friends are and who his family is and he can be at home when he comes back here. He says that's a very secure feeling.'

If Clooney is now secure in his personal life, he is even more settled in his professional life. With *Batman and Robin* now behind him, he seems certain to star in a family film, *Frosty the Snowman*. Based on the famous Christmas song, this is a feature film about a man who comes back from the dead as a snowman to comfort his little boy. In addition to that he may also star in *Out of Sight*. In this adaptation of an Elmore Leonard story Clooney is expected to play a charming robber who escapes from jail and takes a female marshal as a hostage. On top of that he has also written a pilot which has been accepted by NBC as part of his production deal with the network. His biggest role, however, is the lead in an all-star version of *The Thin Red Line*, the prequel to *From Here to Eternity*.

When he got the part in *Batman and Robin* one of the first calls George Clooney made was to his parents. Then just before filming began he called again, as much to prepare them for the media attention as anything else. 'I'm at the top of the roller coaster,' he told them, 'and I can't get off.'

It looks like it'll be some time yet before George Clooney's wild ride hits the buffers.

Index